PENGUIN BUSINESS
FAKE NEWS

Gaurav Sood is a professor of marketing, brand evangelist, researcher, educator, speaker, columnist and author with nearly three decades of practice in creating strong brands. He has been an integral part of developing, and managing marketing and integrated marketing communication campaigns for global brands in India, Germany and the US. He has also carved out a niche for himself as a brand strategist and pioneer in the domain of brand research.

Celebrating 35 Years of
Penguin Random House India

ADVANCE PRAISE FOR THE BOOK

'At a time when fake news has become an unrelenting cancerous spread, Gaurav Sood's book is a valued attempt at analysing the fake news factory, and how it is affecting public discourse. For media practitioners and consumers, the book offers a well-researched insight into just why we need to act before it is too late. A book that diagnoses the problem but also offers solutions. Wish Gaurav all the success!'
—Rajdeep Sardesai, consulting editor, India Today TV

'The publication of *Fake News* is timely and highly relevant, especially as political elections are won or lost today with social media. Gaurav Sood is not only a good scholar but also a master storyteller. His recipe for protecting the brand is very practical! *Fake News* is a must-read for every brand manager'—Professor Jagdish N. Sheth, Goizueta Business School, Emory University, Atlanta, USA

'Gaurav Sood enters a world where factories of image building and image destruction are run. These factories, also known as IT cells in some cases, are organized to create and amplify fake news in order to create a narrative and influence people's perception towards a particular brand or ideology. Gaurav has extensively researched and identified the phenomenon of fake news and its impact and has given solutions to manage the same in his book. This book should be read by every responsible citizen who wants to spot and stop the influence of fake news in their decision-making'—Rana Yashwant, managing editor, India News

'Fake news is a profound problem for civil society worldwide. I have been following Gaurav Sood's work on this topic for some time since his first book, *Troll Proof Branding in the Age of Doppelganger*, was a success and I am impressed by his insights and analysis. In his latest book, he comprehensively discusses the history of fake news, its various facets and how it is spread. He also underlines the impact and implications of fake news on our society and offers valuable suggestions for combatting it. I believe this book is an essential resource for anyone who wants to understand the problem of fake news. It is well-written and informative, providing a valuable perspective on this crucial issue. I highly recommend *Fake News* to anyone interested in understanding and effectively tackling the fake news problem'—Professor Atul Parvatiyar, director, Center for Sales and Customer Relationship Excellence, Rawls College of Business, Texas Tech University

'Gaurav Sood, a friend and professor of marketing has been writing books to bring forward new ideas to contribute to the theory of marketing. His last book, *Troll Proof Branding in the Age of Doppelgangers* was well-researched, insightful and a bestseller, and his new book is timely and important. Gaurav provides a comprehensive overview of the problem of fake news, from its history to its current impact on our society. The book is full of insightful case studies and theories to establish how fake news is used as guerrilla communication. It also dwells on the psychology of fake news and how fake news affects what we buy and consume. While aptly questioning the role of traditional and digital media, he also offers several practical suggestions for how we can spot and combat fake news and protect ourselves from its harmful effects. This book has the potential to help readers understand the problem of fake news and how to combat it. It could also help raise awareness of the issue and encourage people to be more critical of the information that they see online. This book is an essential read for anyone who cares about the future of our information. It is well-written, informative and thought-provoking. I highly recommend it'—Amit Kapoor, honorary chairman, Institute for Competitiveness

'In *Fake News*, Gaurav Sood provides a comprehensive and well-researched overview of the fake news phenomenon. From the ancient history of fake news to the psychology, amplification and role of media in its dissemination and the latest strategies used by its purveyors, this book talks about how fake news is used as a guerrilla communication and how we can protect ourselves from it. The book is a must-read for anyone who wants to understand the threat that fake news poses to our society and how to separate the truth from lies. My best wishes to Gaurav for the success of the book'—Professor Sandeep Puri, Asian Institute of Management, Manila, Philippines

'A fascinating book, *Fake News* is a must-read for everyone, as it has wonderful insights with amazing learnings. The book is quite comprehensive and easy to read'—Professor Varsha Jain, AGK Chair, Mudra Institute of Communication, Ahmedabad

FAKE NEWS
FAKE NEWS
FAKE NEWS
FAKE NEWS
SPOT IT STOP IT

GAURAV SOOD

PENGUIN
BUSINESS

An imprint of Penguin Random House

PENGUIN BUSINESS

USA | Canada | UK | Ireland | Australia
New Zealand | India | South Africa | China | Singapore

Penguin Business is part of the Penguin Random House group of companies
whose addresses can be found at global.penguinrandomhouse.com

Published by Penguin Random House India Pvt. Ltd
4th Floor, Capital Tower 1, MG Road,
Gurugram 122 002, Haryana, India

First published in Penguin Business by Penguin Random House India 2023

ISBN 9780143461319

Typeset in Adobe Caslon Pro by Manipal Technologies Limited, Manipal
Printed at Replika Press Pvt. Ltd, India

www.penguin.co.in

To the ones who love me
and those who fake it

Contents

Contents

I

Fake News—A Guerrilla Communication

'Know when to fight and when not to fight. Avoid what is strong and strike at what is weak. Know how to deceive the enemy: appear weak when you are strong and strong when you are weak.'

—tactics of guerilla warfare summarized
in the sixth-century book *The Art of War*,
by the Chinese general Sun Tzu

It was the tenth day of the Mahabharata war between the Kauravas and Pandavas, the two groups of cousins engaged in a bitter feud for the throne of Hastinapur, a city near the Indian capital of Delhi. The war unfolded in Kurukshetra and served as the backdrop for the Bhagavad Gita—a major Indian philosophical text. Bhishma, the supreme commander of the Kauravas, fell fighting Arjuna, and Guru Dronacharya took his place to lead the Kauravas. The guru assured Duryodhana, the eldest of the Kauravas, that he would capture Yudhishthira, the eldest of the five Pandavas.

Lord Krishna, the Pandavas' adviser, knew it would be difficult to defeat Dronacharya. Aware of the fact that Dronacharya's only weakness was his son Ashwatthama, he came up with a plan to defeat him—by disseminating fake news.

Krishna aimed to demoralize Dronacharya and crush his spirit by creating the false impression that Ashwatthama was killed in fighting. Krishna hoped that the guru would lay down his arms, which would provide them an opportunity to kill him. So, Krishna got Bhima to kill an elephant named after the guru's son and asked him to inform Dronacharya that he had killed Ashwatthama.

On the fourteenth day of the war, Bhima executed Krishna's plan by slaying the elephant and proclaiming that he had killed Ashwatthama. However, Dronacharya, the wise guru that he was, knew of his son's prowess as a warrior and did not believe Bhima's words. He then turned to Yudhishthira, renowned for his adherence to righteousness, and sought confirmation. When asked by Dronacharya if what he heard was true, Yudhishthira affirmed, 'Ashwatthama is dead.' However, he added faintly, 'But it was an elephant and not your son.'

Krishna, aware of Yudhishthira's commitment to the truth, instructed the soldiers to play the trumpets and conches so loudly that the second part of Yudhishthira's sentence would be drowned out. Dronacharya, unable to hear the truth, believed that his son had indeed perished on the battlefield. Krishna's stratagem worked, and Dronacharya, overcome by grief, gave up his weapons and began meditating for his son's soul. Taking advantage of the opportunity, Dhrishtadyumna, the supreme commander of the Pandava army, beheaded the unarmed Dronacharya. Yudhishthira assumed responsibility for this perceived act of deceit throughout his life. Krishna, known for his clever use of strategy, thus successfully used the weapon of misinformation or fake news as a tactic in guerrilla warfare.

According to the Oxford Dictionary, fake news is 'a false report of events written or read on websites'.[1]

Fake news creates significant public confusion regarding current events. Another case of bloodshed caused by fake news can be attributed to the Roman Empire. Almost 2000 years ago, during Julius Caesar's reign, a civil war erupted between Octavian, Caesar's adopted son, and Mark Antony, one of Caesar's loyal and trusted generals. Octavian, who nurtured ambitions of ruling the Roman Empire, knew that to do so, he needed to gather public support to defeat his opponent. Accordingly, he embarked on a campaign of spreading 'fake news' about Mark Antony. Given the absence of newspapers (or any reliable source of information) in that era, Octavian devised a strategy of inscribing coins with concise slogans alleging that Mark Antony was having an affair with Cleopatra, the Egyptian Queen, and that he was a drunkard. The theme of Octavian's misinformation campaign was that Mark Antony, a womanizer and a drunkard, was no more a man of virtue and that by becoming a puppet of Cleopatra, he was no longer fit to govern. Octavian's strategy worked, resulting in him winning the war and enabling him to rule the Roman Empire for many years. Fake news could have also been the reason for Mark Antony's death. Upon hearing of Cleopatra's alleged death, he took his life by impaling himself with a sword. Later on, Cleopatra would also meet a similar fate, resorting to suicide. So, fake news has been employed as a tool or key component of guerrilla communication dating back to 44 BC, or even earlier.

Is this the Art of War? Can opponents, opposition groups, competitors, brands and political activists use fake news to win over their rivals?

The Propaganda War

Even after centuries, 'fake news' has been used as a form of 'guerrilla communication' to harm the reputation of an opponent, political figure, celebrity or brand. It has been used in military and political efforts carefully aimed at spreading fake news and disrupting public opinion. During the Revolutionary War, the revolt of the North American colonies against British rule, Benjamin Franklin created 'fake news' by creating a replica of the *Boston Independent Chronicle* and carrying news of the British wartime atrocities intended to undermine British public support for colonial governance.[2]

Disinformation campaigns were a prominent feature of Cold War espionage. Both the United States and the Soviet Union engaged in covert activities seeking to shape public opinion, destabilize rival governments and gain an edge in the global struggle for power and influence. One of the most effective tools of these covert activities was disinformation, which involved spreading false or misleading information through various channels in order to deceive, confuse or manipulate the public. Disinformation campaigns were used to undermine the credibility of political opponents, sow discord and division within rival societies and create confusion and doubt about the intentions and capabilities of foreign powers. They were often carried out through a variety of channels, including propaganda outlets, forged documents and false rumours spread through social networks and other communication channels. These campaigns were designed to be subtle and nuanced, often using a mix of fact and fiction in order to make the false information seem plausible and believable. While disinformation campaigns have been a feature of espionage and international relations for centuries, the Cold War saw a significant increase in the use of these tactics, as both sides sought to gain the upper hand in the struggle for global dominance. Today, disinformation campaigns remain a common tool of statecraft and political warfare, as governments and other actors seek to shape public opinion and influence the outcomes of domestic and international events.

While traces of fake news can be found in Roman and Indian mythology, its origins can be traced back to the eighteenth century, specifically during the run-up to the American Civil War (1861–65). It was at this time that technological advances in printing fuelled the growth of newspapers, which led to American tabloids fiercely competing for readership. It was during this time that American publisher William Randolph Hearst famously stated, 'War makes for great circulation.'[3]

The war instilled new vigour in journalism, leading to overreach and sensationalization of news. This style became known as 'yellow journalism'. Collins Dictionary defines yellow journalism as 'the type of journalism that relies on sensationalism and lurid exaggeration to attract readers.'[4] A famous example of such journalism was the incident involving the sinking of the battleship USS Maine, on 18 February 1898, in Havana Harbour. Michigan State University discovered that the *New York Journal*, without proper fact-checking or evidence, published a headline pointing fingers at Spain.[5] This instance of misinformation played a part in the outbreak of the Spanish–American War in April 1898, making it a significant piece of yellow journalism during that time.

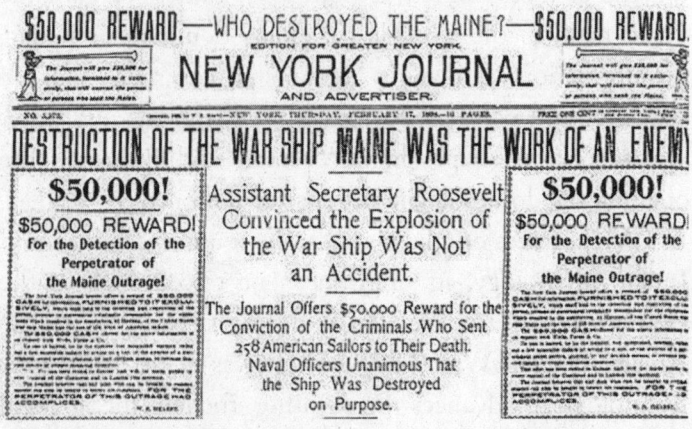

Source: Wikipedia, 'Yellow Journalism'[6]

My book, *Troll Proof Branding in the Age of Doppelgangers*, categorizes fake news into the following types:

1. **Satire or Parody:** stories created with the aim of cultural jamming or creating memes for fun; for example, Charlie Hebdo satirizes issues of public interest.
2. **Misinformation:** selective news coverage of a real event aimed at influencing the perception of the reader or audience in a specific direction.
3. **Biased reporting:** agenda-driven reporting in which facts are not verified or ignored to support a particular position or point of view.
4. **Clickbait:** misleading headlines to attract attention in the digital space to make money or entice users to visit a particular website or landing page.
5. **Propaganda:** stories not based on facts are widely circulated in popular culture to defame a brand or present a brand in an incorrect light.

There are numerous examples throughout history of fake news altering the course of events or influencing the outcome or public perceptions of national importance. This raises an important question—because it is not real, is it dangerous?

Ukraine and Russia's Propaganda War—The Second Front

The Russia–Ukraine war has provided a perfect setting for the dissemination of misinformation, manipulated photos, fake news, state propaganda and fake videos. This quote by Walter Lippmann, American writer, reporter and political commentator, sums up the mindset during times of war: 'We must remember that in time of war what is said on the enemy's side of the front is always propaganda, and what is said on our side of the front is truth and righteousness, the cause of humanity and a crusade for peace.'[7]

A lot of water has flown under the bridge since the onset of the Russia–Ukraine war, which began on 24 February 2022. Since then, infrastructure worth $108 billion (and counting) has been damaged and 3.5 million people have been left homeless on the Ukraine side.[8] The Ukrainian Ministry has assessed, with the help of the Kyiv School of Economics, that 1,40,000 residential buildings, 1,05,200 cars, 43,700 agricultural machines, 764 kindergartens, 1991 shops and 634 cultural facilities have been destroyed by Russian military action. The Russian President, however, would not have expected such resistance to his invasion of Ukraine. Ukraine's President, Volodymyr Zelenskyy, who has film, media and public relations experts on his team, is up against a telegenic opponent in the battle for global support.

The foundation of the Russian–Ukrainian war, or war propaganda, can be traced back to an article written by the Russian President on 12 July 2021 titled 'On the Historical Unity of Russians and Ukrainians'.[9] In this article, Putin highlighted historical links between Russia and Ukraine, and dwelt on how the two countries grew apart with the passage of time. He explained that Russia respected Ukraine's sovereignty and expressed support for Ukrainians given their shared language and culture. However, Putin stated that the new Ukraine, influenced by the West, has adopted an increasingly aggressive approach towards Russia in economic, social, political and spiritual spheres. Putin stated, 'The fact is that the situation in Ukraine today is completely different because it involves a forced change of identity. The most despicable thing is that the Russians in Ukraine are being forced not only to deny their roots, and generations of their ancestors but also to believe that Russia is their enemy. It would not be an exaggeration to say that the path of forced assimilation, the formation of an ethnically pure Ukrainian state, aggressive towards Russia, is comparable in its consequences to the use of weapons of mass destruction against us.'

Condemning the media for terming the invasion a 'war', Putin referred to it as a 'special military action'.

'Faced with the inability of Western countries to negotiate and the Ukrainian Government's war against its people in the east, Russia had no choice but to launch what the Government refers to as its special military operation,' Foreign Minister Sergey Lavrov told the UN General Assembly.

The media's role has remained under scrutiny during the war. While most Russian news channels align with the Kremlin's views on Ukraine, Western media echo the White House's stance. Though the media is capable of countering their government's positions on the war, doing so in Russia can lead to being labelled as anti-national and being imprisoned. For Putin, television matters, and therefore the attack on the Kyiv TV Tower will allow him to control the narrative set for the war. Putin did his best to brainwash the Russians with propaganda and believes that the Ukrainians are fighting back because their government, through TV channels, tells them to do so. Western countries, especially Europe, banned the Russian channel RT and several social media platforms. Google has dropped these channels, including YouTube, from its search and also from the Google Play Store. The media came up with their biased reporting on the Ukraine war refugees, terming them to be closely related to Europeans based on their skin colour and blue eyes, rather than recognizing their origins in countries like Syria or Afghanistan. The fog of propaganda and fake news has heavily influenced the Russia–Ukraine war. The Russians denied that they were at war with Ukraine and said it was just a special military action, and they used fake news as another weapon to fight this war. However, they find it challenging to control the spread of information through citizen journalism and on-the-ground war reporting. On the other hand, Zelenskyy, a professional comedian with little experience in government office before 2019 and limited knowledge of public policy, possesses skilful communication skills, something which has unsettled Putin.[10]

Some of the fake news that has been fact-checked by dw.com on the Russia–Ukraine war:[11]

- **Fact-check: Atrocities in Bucha not 'staged'**
  It is important to acknowledge that there have been reports of civilian deaths and other abuses committed

by Ukrainian forces during the conflict. The incident in Bucha in June 2021, in which five civilians were reportedly killed during a raid by Ukrainian security forces, has been the subject of controversy and allegations of staging. However, dw.com has found these claims to be false.

- **Fact-check: Was a 16-year-old Russian beaten to death by a Ukrainian group in Germany?**
The claim that a 16-year-old Russian died after being attacked by refugees of the Russia–Ukraine war in Germany is false, as no such incident has occurred.

- **Fact-check: Is Russia using butterfly mines in Ukraine?**
There were reports of Russian-backed separatist forces using butterfly mines in Ukraine. Butterfly mines are a type of anti-personnel landmine that are designed to look like harmless objects such as toys or notebooks, remaining hidden for years after deployment. These mines are banned under the Convention on Certain Conventional Weapons (CCW) due to the harm they pose to civilians, but some non-state actors and states have continued to use them. It is important to note that the use of such weapons is a violation of international law and can have severe humanitarian consequences. But the fact check found this story to be false.

The term 'propaganda' is derived from the Latin word 'propagare', which means 'to spread'. Thus, propagandizing means disseminating and spreading a particular idea or ideology. It is a form of guerilla communication encompassing strategies like fake news, lies, manipulation, brainwashing, deceit, psychological warfare and disinformation. As a result, fake news as guerrilla communication is low-cost communication with a specific goal that requires timely imagination and understanding of how your target audience decodes information, by combining existing technologies. It acts as a surgical strike on popular ideology or beliefs and a weapon of psychological warfare to influence the hearts and minds of stakeholders.

Edward Bernays, the father of public relations (PR), used Sigmund Freud's theories on psychological motivation, and rebranded propaganda as public relations. So, propaganda gained legitimacy as a conscious act of persuasion. Every day, PR agencies representing clients actively pursue media houses and journalists to persuade them to highlight their side of the story. Though PR, by definition, is a non-paid form of communication, the influx of money into PR activities for image building of brands has increased over time. It is used to influence public opinion through the media, often being considered more credible than advertising. A PR professional's traditional role was to maintain good relations with journalists to ensure media coverage for their brands. But times have changed. News itself has lost its credibility due to declining readership or the credibility of news channels. It is difficult to say, but state and corporate interference has made news more profit-oriented and is also perceived as pushing the state's agenda. Newspaper sales in the United

States are nearly half of what they were in 1994, and the pandemic has slowed the growth of the print media even further. Propaganda is used not only in war or as a public relations exercise, but also in advertising, where testimonials, bandwagoning, stereotyping, fear appeals, name-calling and other methods of persuasion are used to influence consumer perception of the brand.

In war, particularly when dealing with a formidable opponent who poses a threat to your existence or growth, fake news is used as a guerrilla tactic to undermine the opponent's strategies. Digital technology has made fake news as a tool faster, more cost-effective and with a wider reach.

War Propaganda Programming[12]

1. Start with the coverage and use visuals from the most recent wars.
2. Plan and prepare the public for war, portraying leaders as dangerous figures and a threat to the world.
3. Record and share stories and visual documentation of the ongoing war, domestic public reactions, global media bytes, international support and predictions of what a post-war scenario will look like.
4. Follow media reactions and manage them, and analyse the impact of government restrictions and their impact due to the war.
5. Manage academic reactions and public opinion which oppose the war and term it as unnecessary.
6. Start with Step 1 for the next war.

While propaganda can be used in many different contexts, including advertising and political campaigns, it has also been used as a tool of warfare and conquest throughout history. One of the most notorious examples of propaganda used to invade a sovereign country is evident in Nazi Germany's actions leading up to and during World War II. The Nazi regime used propaganda to demonize Jews and other groups, to justify their aggression towards neighbouring countries and to rally support for their war efforts. More recently, there have been allegations that propaganda and fake news have been used in various conflicts and political crises around the world. For example, some have accused Russia of using propaganda to influence the outcome of the 2016 US presidential election, as well as to sow division and confusion in other countries. Similarly, there have been allegations of propaganda and disinformation being used in conflicts in Syria and Ukraine.

So, we see how propaganda, a form of fake news, has been used to invade sovereign countries and disturb power dynamics in a geographical region. Another tactic is to exploit 'fear' as an emotional platform to show terrorism as a threat to a community or a nation that cares for its citizens. By fostering fear, people are led to believe in the narrative of a 'War on Terrorism' and perceive the enemy as an 'axis of evil'.

Fake News as a Guerrilla Warfare Tool

Fake news is a form of guerrilla warfare as it matches the strategies and tactics used to fight a formidable enemy. So why use fake news as a guerrilla warfare tool? Guerrilla warfare has a long history; one finds instances of it recorded in the Bible. Propaganda, an important strategy in war, is a form of fake news. According to the Cambridge Dictionary, propaganda is defined as 'information, ideas, opinions, or images, often only giving one part of an argument, that are broadcast, published, or in some other way spread with the intention of influencing people's opinions'.

Propaganda is inherently controversial as it is deployed as a strategy to influence audience behaviour and attitudes in times of war or now as fake news to vilify people, policies, brands and issues. There are numerous examples of how propaganda is used to justify war or influence the war outcome.

America justified its invasion of Iraq to the American public through a well-orchestrated strategic propaganda campaign executed via mass media. The Iraq war questions the role of the media, which challenges the sociological theory that intends to consider, analyse and/or explain objects of social reality from a sociological perspective. According to Jeremy Browne, former foreign office minister in the UK government, 'In democracies, the media is fundamental to political life. It provides facts to allow us to be better informed about the issues that matter to us. It provides criticism and debate to ensure that that information is tested and examined from all points of view.'[13] However, due to competitive pressures and the race for higher television ratings (Television Rating Points or TRP), as well as toeing the line of the ruling party for which they are labelled as 'Godi media' (lapdogs of the ruling party) in India, the television media become a delivery vehicle for propaganda to fuel public passion and provide legitimacy to government policies. The Iraq war is a great example of the role of the media in spreading misinformation.

On 20 March 2003, the world witnessed how propaganda can lead to a war between sovereign nations when the United States of America invaded Iraq. America was bruised by the attack on the Twin Towers of the World Trade Center, which symbolized America's global influence, economic power and prosperity. The Bush administration used the media to legitimize their narrative, aimed at implicating Iraq's President Saddam Hussein for the 9/11 attack. They claimed that the Iraqi government was not cooperating with the United Nations for weapons inspection and that America was aware that they were hiding weapons of mass destruction (WMD) which could be used against America or could land in the hands of terrorists. The American and the international media supported this and ignored any contradictory views on the topic, and later it was found that all the American claims were wrong. The American public was taken for a ride through this war propaganda, and subsequently, the public became less supportive of President Bush's claims of WMDs and justification for the invasion of Iraq.

The American public is largely dependent on TV and newspapers for their consumption of international news, but the American media did not bring forward important contextual and background information on the social and political situation in the Middle East, which led to the Iraq war. The only agenda the media followed was to create a narrative of the 'War on Terrorism' after the 9/11 attack. This was part of a larger story that included the hunt for Al-Qaeda leaders, invading Afghanistan and expanding US military presence around the world. Sociologists from Arizona State University have drawn a conceptual schema of the propaganda war on Iraq.

A Threat to Democracy

Democracy both in America and India has been compromised by new-age technology, particularly social media platforms, cheap newsprint and the presence of the 'Godi' media—outlets that are perceived to be 'sitting in the lap of the government or the ruling party'.[14] These developments have led to concerns about biased journalism and have shaken the foundations of the fourth pillar of democracy. The reputation of journalism has been compromised, leading to the spread of misinformation and a reduction in substantive policy debates. Content can be posted by users without any substantial credentials, which can further be amplified by many on social media platforms like Facebook and Twitter (now X) without any fact-checking, filtration or editorial judgement. These tweets or posts can have a reach comparable to any traditional news channel, influencing people's perceptions and damaging the reputation of the targeted subject.

The term 'fake news' gained popularity during the 2016 US presidential election when Cambridge Analytica was accused of 'micro-targeting' Facebook users who happened to be US voters. Around 32,000 US voters were paid $2 to $5 in order to take a personality or political preference test.[15] These voters were required to take that test by registering with their Facebook accounts. Hence, Cambridge Analytica got default access to 32,000 voters' personal political preferences as expressed by them on their Facebook profiles through 'likes' and 'posts'. Not only did the company gain access to the data of 32,000 Facebook users, but they also gained access to their friends' Facebook data, totalling over 50 million users. Then, Cambridge Analytica compared the personality test results with the users' Facebook activities and created a psychological profile of the user. Further, the company integrated user data from other sources like voter records, and with the help of algorithms, was able to create hundreds of data points for a single user or voter. These data points were used to micro-target these users with highly targeted political campaigns to swing their preference towards a particular party ideology.

The data analytics teams worked with Donald Trump's election team and the Brexit campaign to develop psychographic profiling of millions of Facebook profiles of US voters. This was the biggest data breach in Facebook's history, as it involved the illegal use of user data to predict and influence choices and voting patterns in the US presidential election. The whistle-blower from Cambridge Analytica revealed that they exploited Facebook to harvest millions of people's profiles and built models to exploit the information they had in order to target individuals' vulnerabilities. This approach was the foundation on which the company was built.

Random likes of Facebook users can be used to develop complex character assessments through psychological profiling and create Facebook users' personality traits. These personality traits were based on the OCEAN model (openness, conscientiousness, extraversion, agreeableness, and neuroticism), the 'Big 5' personality traits. Statistical tools and algorithms used to predict individuals' attributes from their digital footprints and behaviour are a breach of their privacy, and such captured individual data can be applied to large sets of individual data to develop a pattern without the individuals' consent. How Cambridge Analytica gathered the data of 50 million Facebook users can be explained in the figure below:

As a result, the phenomenon of fake news not only affects Western countries, but it is also prevalent in India. In 2020, India's stalwart Indian industrialist, philanthropist and former chairman of Tata Sons, Ratan Tata, came out on Twitter denying viral fake news claims that he had predicted a huge fall in the Indian economy due to COVID-19.

Personality Test — paid $2-5 to take a detailed personality/political test

User Data — collected data such as likes and personal information

Likes
- personality quiz results were paired with their Facebook data – such as likes – to seek out psychological patterns

highly personalised advertising
- Algorithms combined the data with other sources such as voter records to create a superior set of records

Source: *Troll Proof Branding in the Age of Doppelgangers* by Gaurav Sood (2022)

Ratan N. Tata ✓
@RNTata2000   ...

This post has neither been said, nor written by me. I urge
you to verify media circulated on WhatsApp and social
platforms. If I have something to say, I will say it on my
official channels. Hope you are safe and do take care.

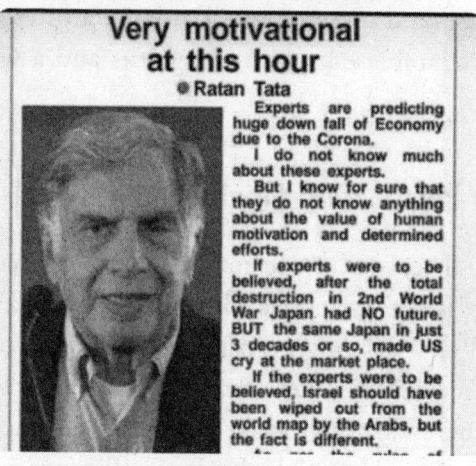

Very motivational at this hour
● Ratan Tata

Experts are predicting huge down fall of Economy due to the Corona.

I do not know much about these experts.

But I know for sure that they do not know anything about the value of human motivation and determined efforts.

If experts were to be believed, after the total destruction in 2nd World War Japan had NO future. BUT the same Japan in just 3 decades or so, made US cry at the market place.

If the experts were to be believed, Israel should have been wiped out from the world map by the Arabs, but the fact is different.

Source: Twitter, Ratan N. Tata[16]

This highlights the manner in which fake news has
been used as a guerrilla communication strategy, aimed at
adversely impacting the democratic processes of nations.
The term 'guerrilla' conjures up images of unconventional
conflicts, rebels and the unorthodox combative nature
of communication. The term 'guerrilla communication'
seems to have been derived from Jay Conrad Levinson's
1984 book 'Guerrilla Marketing'. According to Levinson,
companies use unconventional methods of marketing and
communication to drive sales and increase market share.
Guerrilla tactics are based on surprising your opponent

with unconventional methods of combat. It is based on short and sudden ambushes to destroy, damage or obstruct for political, business or military advantage. Fake news is one such unconventional tactic or tool to destroy or build a brand's reputation. Truth, an arbiter of reality, is a sacred, unbiased, unwavering lens and a window to the world.

Partisan Polarization Driving Fake News

In 2020, there was a rise in fake news on social media targeting Rahul Gandhi's Bharat Jodo Yatra (Uniting India Rally). The Congress party—India's main opposition party—claimed that the rally was the longest to be ever undertaken by any politician, covering a distance of 3750 km from Kanyakumari to Kashmir. The *padayatra* (foot march) was a protest against the 'politics of fear, bigotry, and prejudice' and against the economics of livelihood destruction, increasing unemployment and growing inequalities. As the rally gained momentum and popularity, it became a target for fake news and baseless allegations aimed at destabilizing its purpose and discrediting its goals. Among those who spread fake news about the rally was Priti Gandhi, a social media baiter who mistook Congress youth party worker Miva Jolly for Amulya Noronha, who had raised pro-Pakistan slogans during a protest against the Citizenship Amendment Bill (CAA). Priti Gandhi claimed in her tweet that this is no 'Bharat Jodo Yatra' but a 'Bharat Todo Yatra' (Dividing India Rally).

Priti Gandhi - प्रीति गांधी ✓
@MrsGandhi

Look carefully. Not Bharat Jodo, this is Bharat Todo!!

0:18

86 views

1:31 AM · 24 Sep 22 · Twitter for Android

11 Retweets **32** Likes

Source: Twitter, Priti Gandhi[17]

Initially, when the rally started, BJP minister Smriti Irani accused Rahul Gandhi of not paying tributes to Swami Vivekananda at the Vivekananda Rock memorial. This also turned out to be a false claim as the Congress leader had visited the memorial and paid tribute to Vivekananda before commencing his rally. The Congress party is believed to have taken legal action against those who spread the fake allegations and is said to be vigilant against malicious insinuations that tried to undo the progress that the Congress leader had achieved through his rally.

Tool without a Handle

The proliferation of news sources and the presence of satire, as well as the ease and speed of social media, combined with readers' short attention spans and a tendency to just breeze through the headlines, create an environment where it is easy for readers to fall for fake news. Some websites have taken it upon themselves to fact-check rumours, health claims and political claims—particularly those that show up often on social media. These are mostly American and Chinese companies dominating the digital space. It is hard to imagine that Google and Facebook alone have an 84 per cent share in the world's advertising market. Facebook, which has more than two billion users, makes a whopping 55 billion dollars from advertisements alone.

It is hard to figure out if these companies are media platforms or advertising companies. These tech companies have destroyed the news industry by invading editorial space and showing scant regard for the health and freedom of the news pipeline. These pseudo-newsrooms, which sit on massive platforms, focus on hypersensitive community stories. They do not go beyond what their backers want them to. It is said that patronizing goes hand in hand with fake news. The elephant in the room is the advertising market and its influence on the funding of fake news busters. The past few years have seen a burgeoning of news sites that are part of the clickbait circuit, which is a mechanism to spread false and misleading advertisements. The fake-news circuit is typically 24 hours long and, in some cases, corrects itself only to deliberately create a backlash, just enough to secure more clicks.

Fake news has become a pervasive phenomenon. It is being used as a tool to advance partisan agendas worldwide. The crisis of fake news is particularly severe in India, a country with a vast population and diverse social, political and religious beliefs. Social media platforms have become popular in India, and their reach has been on the rise for the last few years, with an estimated user count of 376 million. Unfortunately, this has also led to an increase in the spread of fake news and misinformation.

The spread of fake news in India has had serious consequences, such as inciting communal violence, spreading rumours about public health issues and influencing political opinion. In recent years, fake news has played a significant role in fuelling mob violence, lynching and riots in various parts of India. Moreover, during the COVID-19 pandemic, fake news and misinformation on social media caused panic among the public and hindered the efforts of the government to effectively contain the spread of the virus.

The Indian government has taken steps to tackle the spread of fake news and misinformation, such as introducing laws to regulate social media platforms, including WhatsApp, which is a popular platform for spreading fake news in India. However, the problem persists, and there is a need for collaborative efforts that would include the government, social media platforms and civil society to combat the crisis of fake news in India. The goal is not only to investigate the devastating effects of fake news on society, individuals and brands but also to understand its origins and dissemination in order to devise strategies to eliminate fake news from our lives.

People might have fallen for fake news, but it is not solely their fault. While individuals do bear some responsibility in verifying the information they consume, there are several factors that contribute to the spread of fake news and misinformation. Firstly, fake news can be designed to look and sound convincing, making it difficult for people to identify it as false. In some cases, fake news can be intentionally misleading and designed to prey on people's biases and emotions, making it even harder for individuals to recognize it as false. Secondly, social media algorithms and echo chambers can create a feedback loop where people are only exposed to information that confirms their existing beliefs and biases. This can make it difficult for people to view a situation from different perspectives or to question the accuracy of information that aligns with their existing beliefs. Lastly, the widespread distribution of fake news can be attributed to the lack of regulation and oversight on social media platforms. Social media platforms have been criticized for not doing enough to combat the spread of fake news and misinformation, and this lack of action can contribute to the problem.

On 4 December 2016, a 28-year-old man, a father of two, believed what he had read online, that Comet Ping Pong, a pizza restaurant in northwest Washington, was running a racket of young children as sex slaves, and that this racket was led by none other than presidential candidate Hillary Clinton. The gentleman drove for six hours carrying his assault rifle to investigate if this news was true.[18] He reached the pizzeria and fired some gunshots, which hit the ceiling, hurting no one. He later realized that the reports were blatantly untrue. Later, he was arrested and charged with four counts, including felony, assault with a deadly weapon, and carrying a gun without a licence outside a home or business.

Unsurprisingly, this man was not the only one who fell for the fake news, which had by then been widely circulated on social media and was consumed by many others like him. Collectively, they all started believing that the Washington pizzeria was the headquarters of a child trafficking ring run by Hillary Clinton. The article was soon condemned by the *New York Times*, *Washington Post* and fact-checking site Snopes as 'fake news'. But Comet Ping Pong's problems were far from over, as it faced consumer backlash on Facebook, Twitter and Instagram. The owner of Comet Ping Pong saw his pizzeria as the victim of a targeted fake news campaign and closed his restaurant for a few days for tensions to ease. He later released a statement, saying, 'We should all condemn the efforts of certain people to spread malicious and utterly false accusations about Comet Ping Pong.'

Pizzagate, as they call it, is just the tip of the iceberg of controversies created by fake news. Recent years have seen some major events—the US presidential election, Cambridge Analytica and Facebook scandal, the outbreak of the COVID-19 pandemic, the Russia–Ukraine war, the India–China border standoff, and Bollywood drug incidents including Sushant Singh Rajput's death and Aryan Khan's cruise controversy, to name a few. While these incidents were covered extensively by the media across the world, there were clear instances where the media overstepped and spread misleading or false information. Of all these events, the one which threatens the democracy of a sovereign nation is the biggest damage that fake news can do.

Digitalization of Guerrilla Communication

News is a public good that has to be handled with care and integrity. Lies and misinformation campaigns have been around for years, maybe since the dawn of journalism. However, the rate at which fake news is being spread these days is both alarming and preposterous. Almost every institution—public or private—uses fake news to further its agenda. Governments and corporate houses spread fake news either through their own agencies or by influencing popular media. In the business sector, fake news manifests itself in the form of exaggerated company returns and false data. Fake political news is the new yellow. Just like yellow journalism in the late nineteenth and early twentieth centuries, fake political news is often sensationalistic, biased and deliberately misleading. It is designed to grab people's attention and generate clicks and shares, regardless of whether or not the information is accurate.

From Donald Trump to Narendra Modi, from war propaganda to the Coronavirus, and from epics like the Mahabharata to historical figures such as Julius Caesar, the existence of 'fake news' or fabricated news can be traced back to as far as mankind can remember. Since then, it has become such a powerful tool to spread misinformation and rumours to destroy a brand image and create a brand doppelgänger. Fake news in recent years has been the most talked about topic, and it has become difficult to differentiate between the truth and a lie. The popularity of the term 'fake news' is so great that in the year 2017, it became the 'word of the year' in the Collins Dictionary. Though we might have come to know of this term only recently, its examples abound throughout ancient history. From ancient Rome to India, fake news has misled regimes, countries, leaderships, people and consumers. It has been used for financial manipulation, influencing perceptions and destroying faith and trust. Many of us seem unable to distinguish fake news from the verified sort. Fake news creates significant public confusion about current events.

There are reports suggesting how misinformation played a critical role in the election of Donald Trump as the president of the US. The crisis of fake news, however, is much more severe in India, all because of the large number of social media users and poor regulation of social media by the government. India is an attractive market due to its large consumer base and internet penetration, which make it a happy hunting ground for social media platforms. However, due to low literacy and digital media literacy rates as compared to other countries, India is more vulnerable to fake news. Tampered videos and fake news are rampant on social media platforms like WhatsApp, Facebook and Twitter, sometimes resulting in communal disharmony and social tensions.

In today's media landscape, both traditional and digital, finding 'truth' has become an uphill task. The overflow of misinformation sometimes obscures the truth, making it difficult to determine what is genuine and what is fake. As a result, citizens and consumers are left more confused than ever as they have to choose which brand to buy, what party to vote for, which ideology to follow, what to believe and what not to. This is what fake news has done to us, emerging as a popular but perilous phenomenon.

In the digital world, fake news is a powerful and socially destructive force. It has a global reach and widespread vulnerability. This is why it is important to understand why and how fake news is created, spread and—most importantly—combatted.

Social media platforms, such as Facebook, use audience-targeted advertising based on parameters like demography, geography, location, interest and devices. Now, this can be a threat to democracy as social media can change people's political preferences as audience targeting can segment the social media users based on their profiles, compatible views or confirmation biases. So, if political parties only target a subset of voters with their advertisements, how can the issues raised by the advertisements be debated openly? Also, how can other parties get an opportunity to counter the argument and how can the media question the claims made in the advertisement? Every political party releases its manifesto ahead of the elections and makes several promises. If they are made in private, through social media messages, which can distort perceptions or swing votes, then how can the party be held accountable for the same?

Modern digital marketing campaigns target us in such a way that we are shown ads based on our personal data or psychographic profiles. Since we prefer to see certain types or categories of videos or views supporting a political party, social media platforms show us more of such content linked to our confirmation bias. So, a user sees a particular advertisement only because he or she has been profiled to watch that content even if the person has not subscribed to nor given his consent to view such content. The social media algorithms are designed in such a way that you can clearly see a pattern which exists in the kind of content we are exposed to. Until a different type of content emerges, maybe in the form of communication from an opposition party, we'll be limited in our understanding of the real issues and will see only one side of the argument. This will distort our information processing system and we will not make a logically sound decision.

As we know, fake news is a false report of events written or read on websites. But is that enough for us to know about this 'optimized disinformation' phenomenon? Well, it has acquired a thin layer of legitimacy by rewriting truth

or misrepresenting facts in a completely believable way
through advertising, clickbait headlines, memes, parody,
manipulation, political satire, biased news reporting and
propaganda. Fake news is used to manipulate beliefs,
perceptions, motivations and actions of individuals or
groups of like-minded individuals. Added to this is the role
of social media in amplifying or acting as a delivery vehicle
for fake news, a new form of guerrilla communication.
Those who use fake news as a guerrilla communication tool
believe they can win the war by any means and at any cost.
So, is 'fake it to make it' the new normal?

II

Fake News—A Tool for
Culture Jamming

'Culture jamming is enjoying a resurgence, in part
because of technological advancements but also more
pertinently, because of the good old rules of supply and
demand. Something not far from the surface of the public
psyche is delighted to see the icons of corporate power
subverted and mocked. There is, in short, a market for
it. With commercialism able to overpower the traditional
authority of religion, politics and schools, corporations
have emerged as the natural targets for all sorts of free-
floating rage and rebellion. The new ethos that culture
jamming taps into is go-for-the-corporate-jugular.'

—Naomi Klein, *No Logo*

In her bestselling book *No Logo*—which she declares the
next political movement—author Naomi Klein takes aim
at big brands like Microsoft, Starbucks, Nike and Pepsi,

as well as celebrities, political parties and public policies which find themselves under attack by political activists, brand activists and consumers on a large scale. These brands advocate how their products, ideas and ideologies can change the way we live but their communications are subverted and mocked by culture jammers. Culture Jamming is defined by dictionary.com as 'a form of political and social activism which, by means of fake adverts, hoax news stories, pastiches of company logos and product labels, computer hacking, etc., draws attention to and at the same time subverts the power of the media, governments, and large corporations to control and distort the information that they give to the public in order to promote consumerism, militarism, etc.'[1]

Culture jamming is another form of guerilla communication used to expose the methods of control exerted by governments, mainstream cultural and social institutions and corporate firms. Generally, it is a form of protest carried out by anti-establishment groups or anti-brand activists against government policies and corporate practices.

Fake news is a prominent feature of culture jamming, used to build a counter-narrative by critiquing elements of consumer culture through hijacking, deconstructing and repurposing. According to Mark Dery (1993), it can take many forms:[2]

1. Sniping and Subvertising
2. Adbusters

3. Media Fake News
4. Audio Propaganda
5. Billboard Banditry
6. Guerrilla Semiotics
7. Postscript from the edge

An example of culture jamming using billboards as a form of protest can be seen in the movie 'Three Billboards Outside Ebbing, Missouri', in which Frances McDormand plays a divorced mother whose daughter has been raped and killed a year ago, with the case remaining unsolved. In her quest for justice, she uses three billboards to demand that the authorities solve the case and bring the perpetrators to justice. The three billboards not only attracted media attention but also sparked a debate that put pressure on the police to solve the case. This is an example of using billboards as a guerilla communication to protest against state authority and garner public and media attention towards a cause. Frances's performance won her the Academy Award for Best Actress in a Leading Role, as she portrayed a character who confronts the authority for being unfair and denying her justice. Billboard Banditry was common in the 1970s and 1980s with a group of culture jammers calling themselves BUGAUP (Billboard Utilizing Graffitists Against Unhealthy Promotions) who protested by placing anti-tobacco messages on billboards. BUGAUP can be known as the pioneer of this kind of culture jamming.

'NO WAR'

On 20 March 2003, a US-led coalition launched an invasion of Iraq, sparking widespread condemnation against the aggression. In Australia, two people came up with a novel way to register their protest against the invasion. They scaled to the top of the Sydney Opera House, to its highest sail, and painted the words 'NO WAR'. This message went viral, with pictures of the act being broadcast across the world. Though the individuals behind the protest were arrested and fined, their act inspired other activists to take this campaign forward by painting 'NO WAR' on any picture they came across of the Sydney Opera House.

Source:

Image © Dean Sewell, from the exhibition Culture Jammers at the Museum of Sydney [3]

This unique way of protesting is known as culture jamming, which has been used to disrupt communication within popular culture. Fake news is one such tool which can be used to disrupt information which is disseminated for public consumption. Fake news is impacting people powerfully, blurring their ability to tell the truth from lies. An example of how the mainstream media becomes entangled in spreading fake news is the polygamy hoax that originated in Iraq and spread to four different countries. The fake news was that the government of Eritrea had mandated men to have two wives. This false claim was propagated by mainstream media in Kenya, Nigeria, Eritrea and Sudan, confusing people who believed it to be true, particularly when it came from their trusted media outlets. The hoax spread further on social media, prompting the Eritrean embassy to term it 'appalling'.[4]

Fake news is deliberately designed to deceive the public, diverting their attention from the real issues and to manipulate the media, government, corporations or famous personalities. This is a form of culture jamming that is dangerous to journalism at large. It's an information disorder ranging from disinformation to misinformation.

Fake News—Culture Jamming the Democratic Process

Fake news poses a threat to democracy and effective governance. Fake news alters facts and influences opinion, disrupts the organic processes of public opinion formation, and can influence voting patterns by twisting the truth. Fake news develops and circulates false narratives, creates confusion and doubts, leads to social polarization and induces selective bias, disrupting the democratic process of decision-making. When fake news is used as a tool for culture jamming, it can be particularly effective in shaping public opinion and influencing political outcomes. By spreading false or misleading information, culture jammers can create confusion and sow distrust in mainstream news sources, making it more difficult for voters to make informed decisions. In recent years, the issue of fake news has become increasingly prominent, with many governments and organizations around the world taking steps to combat it. This includes measures such as fact-checking initiatives, media literacy programmes and increased regulation of social media platforms. Ultimately, the spread of fake news and the use of culture jamming as a tool for manipulating public opinion represents a serious threat to the democratic process. It is up to all of us, as individuals and as a society, to remain vigilant against these practices and to work towards promoting transparency, accuracy and accountability in the media and in our political discourse.

In the 2016 US presidential election, fake news emerged as a powerful and sinister force that heavily influenced the transparency of the voting process. Fake news, due to its captivating nature, is more attention-grabbing than real news. A group of activists in the US created a website called 'Hacking Hillary', which claimed to have evidence of corruption and illegal activities by then-presidential candidate Hillary Clinton. The website, carefully crafted to look like a legitimate source of news, spread false information about Clinton's alleged wrongdoings in an attempt to discredit her campaign. The creators of the website later admitted that it was a form of culture jamming, intended to draw attention to the problem of fake news and propaganda in the political sphere.[5] However, the use of fake news in this context was still controversial and potentially damaging, as it contributed to the spread of false information and undermined public trust in the democratic process.

A Buzzfeed News analysis shows that the fake news generated during the 2016 US presidential election got more engagement on Facebook than all major mainline media sources combined, including reputable outlets such as the *New York Times*, *Washington Post*, *Huffington Post* and NBC News.[6] The fake news originated from hoax websites and hyperpartisan blogs, and was amplified with numerous shares, comments and likes on Facebook, resulting in the platform gaining a reputation for being a delivery vehicle for fake news. Native videos, live content and image posts got the most traction on Facebook, and the top stories were just a fraction of the overall engagement of fake news on Facebook. According to Buzzfeed News, the top five fake election stories by Facebook engagements (total number of shares, reactions and comments) just three months before the elections were:[7]

1. 'Pope Francis Shocks World, Endorses Donald Trump for President'—960,000 engagements

2. 'WikiLeaks Confirms Hillary Clinton Sold Weapons to ISIS. Then Drops Another Bombshell! Breaking News'—789,000 engagements

3. 'It's Over: Hillary's ISIS Email Just Leaked & It's Worse Than Anyone Could Have Imagined'—754,000 engagements

4. 'Just Read The Law: Hillary Is Disqualified From Holding Any Federal Office'—701,000 engagements

5. 'FBI Agent Suspected In Hillary Email Leaks Found Dead In Apparent Murder Suicide'—567,000 engagements.

Whereas, the top five mainline election stories by Facebook engagements included:

1. 'Trump's history of corruption is mind-boggling. So, why is Clinton supposedly the corrupt one?'—*Washington Post*, 849,000 engagements.

2. 'Stop pretending you don't know why people hate Hillary Clinton'—*Huffington Post*, 623,000 engagements

3. 'Melania Trump's girl-on-girl photos from racy shoot revealed'—*New York Post*, 531,000 engagements

4. 'Ford fact-checks Trump: we will be here forever'—CNN, 407,000 engagements

5. 'I ran the CIA. Now I am endorsing Hillary Clinton'—*New York Times*, 373,000 engagements.

This shows how insidious fake news can be. Blame it on social media to amplify its overall effect on the US presidential election and voters' electoral choices.

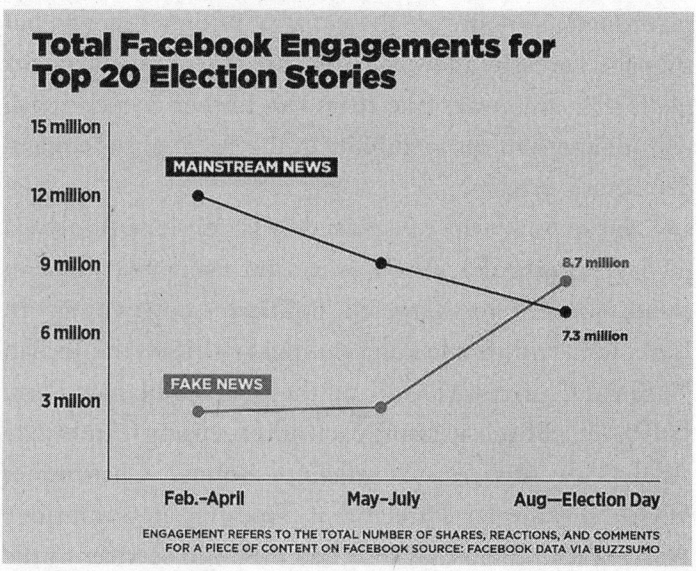

Total Facebook Engagements for Top 20 Election Stories

ENGAGEMENT REFERS TO THE TOTAL NUMBER OF SHARES, REACTIONS, AND COMMENTS FOR A PIECE OF CONTENT ON FACEBOOK SOURCE: FACEBOOK DATA VIA BUZZSUMO

Source: Buzzfeed News[8]

Fake news transcends political lines and geographical boundaries, and the current political landscape gives way to the creation and amplification of misinformation on social media platforms. This has resulted in an erosion of the credibility of mainstream media and has left audiences further polarized. Consequently, fake news has become a vital part of political strategies and has been used as a tool by political parties against each other. While fake news existed before the advent of modern politics, digital mediums have made it socially engaging as almost everyone is a media outlet and can share and spread false information. Finneman and Thomas (2018) attribute the rise of fake news to the rise of the internet, particularly social media platforms.[9] Not only are these platforms user-friendly, but they also are easily affordable compared to traditional media platforms. This way, fake news can further deepen social discord and ruin the credibility of the electoral system and democratic principles.

Not to forget the role played by Cambridge Analytica in data-mining Facebook users and using that data to create profiles for targeted political campaigning. In India too, both the leading political parties—the Indian National Congress (INC) and the Bharatiya Janata Party (BJP)—have been accusing each other of using Cambridge Analytica's services to influence voters. Christopher Wylie, the former Director of Research at Cambridge Analytica, testified that they had provided services to the Congress party in India. Another report suggests that the BJP had been using the services of the SCL Group, the parent company of Cambridge Analytica, during the run-up to the 2014 elections, which they ended up sweeping.[10]

The question arises: is it fair to use such strategies for political gain? From the perspective of a marketer, one might agree, but such methods do more harm than good by exploiting the vulnerabilities of those who are susceptible to fake news. These targeted campaigns exploit sensitive issues like religion, caste, minority rights, nationalism and probably poverty while simultaneously maligning the image of the Opposition and its leadership. India finds itself in a precarious state of digital revolution, thanks to a combination of low literacy and emotional decision-making. So, anything that is attractive is accepted as the truth, resulting in a highly politically polarized public.

Fake News—Manipulating People's Perception of Reality

The danger of fake news lies in its ability to manipulate people's perception of reality. By presenting false information as the truth, fake news can shape people's beliefs, attitudes and behaviours, leading to confusion, fear and even harm. For example, fake news can be used to influence people's political views by spreading false information about candidates or issues. It can also be used to promote dangerous health practices or conspiracy theories that could harm individuals or communities. It is important to be critical of the information we receive and verify it from reliable sources before accepting it as true. By being vigilant and checking sources, we can help prevent the spread of fake news and protect ourselves and our communities from its harmful effects.

Many current events have been culture-jammed by fake news to dilute their intensity. In 2020, the Indian government introduced new farm laws, triggering nationwide protests by farmers. They demanded the repeal of these laws as they believed that they favoured the big corporations and were detrimental to the interests of farmers. As the farmer agitation gained momentum and encircled Delhi, the capital of India, fake news started doing the rounds on social media. Though many fake reports gained traction on social media, here are a few worth mentioning:[11]

1. An image of Canadian Prime Minister Justin Trudeau with the Sikh community was circulated, falsely claiming his participation in the farmers' protest.
2. An old photograph showing police using water cannons to disperse the farmers was shared by prominent personalities. It was later revealed to be fake.
3. An old image was shared claiming that the farmers were also protesting for the restoration of Article 370 in Kashmir.
4. An old image of a banner condemning Indian Prime Minister Narendra Modi and Uttar Pradesh Chief Minister Yogi Adityanath was shared, implying that it was from the farmers' protest. Later, this proved to be false.

Boom, a fact-checking website, debunked several fake images associated with Rahul Gandhi's 'Bharat Jodo Yatra'. These fake images included:[12]

1. A comical fake image of Union Minister Smriti Irani watching Rahul Gandhi's 'Bharat Jodo Yatra' on her laptop.
2. Misleading images of Rahul Gandhi holding hands with his niece, presented with false claims.
3. A morphed photograph of Rahul Gandhi having tea and what was claimed to be a beef dish, whereas the original picture did not have the plate of beef.

4. An image of Rahul Gandhi hugging a girl, falsely claimed to be Amulya Leona Noronha who raised the 'Pakistan Zindabad' slogan in February 2020, when it was in fact a member of the Kerala Student Union

Fake News: Culture Jamming the Celebrities

Fake news and celebrities have a weird relationship. Love them or hate them, but you can't ignore them. Peeping into the lives of these celebrities and following them on social media has become a ritual for millions of fans worldwide. There was a time when these celebrities seemed unreachable and could only be idolized by their fans on the small or big screen. Now, they are ever so accessible through social media that you can not only get daily feeds from them about their lives but also have an opportunity to interact with them directly. Fans and followers now have the opportunity to see the stars beyond their screen characters, making them feel more connected. Fans learn about their daily routines and emotions through their posts. Also, social media offers instant access to any news related to these celebrities, usually much faster than traditional media platforms like newspapers or television.

However, all that is posted on social media about your favourite celebrity may not be true. Fake news is deliberately circulated to deceive readers by fabricating stories in a way that makes them believable. The stories are built around the celebrity's life and are based on certain other events or circumstances at that time. An example of this is the spread of fake news concerning the Johnny Depp–Amber Heard defamation trial in the United States. One such fake news claim is that Amber Heard's opening quote is a straight lift from the character Marge Sherwood in the famous 1999 American psychological thriller movie *The Talented Mr. Ripley*. The opening lines read as follows:

'The thing with Johnny . . . it's like the sun shines on you, and it's glorious. And then he forgets you and it's very, very cold.'

'When you have his attention, you feel like you're the only person in the world, that's why everybody loves him so much.'

These lines may be inspired by the movie, but not a rip-off from it.[13] Another fake news story that emerged during the trial suggested that 'Amber Heard snorted cocaine while on the stand giving her testimony'. This was analysed by forensic behavioural experts, who found no evidence of such behaviour in the trial video.[14] She just happened to be using tissue paper from the table, and there was no evidence of misuse or abuse.

Another example of celebrity fake news is when an entertainment portal named Pinkvilla claimed that Indian actor Arjun Kapoor and Malaika Arora were planning their first child and that she was pregnant. A furious Arjun Kapoor posted the following message on Instagram: '@ pinkvilla and journalist Nikita Dalvi—this is the lowest that you could have gone and you have done it by being casual, insensitive and absolutely unethical in carrying garbage news. This journalist has been writing such pieces regularly and getting away with it because we tend to ignore these fake gossip articles while they spread across media and become the truth. This is not done. Don't dare to play with our personal lives.'[15]

Source: 'Arjun Kapoor Calls Report of 'Malaika Arora's Pregnancy "GARBAGE"', NewsroomPost.[16]

ExpressVPN, a virtual private network, used Linkfluence, a platform for monitoring online conversations, to research the association of the phrase 'fake news' with celebrities, politicians and public figures. While the news, be it real or fake, mostly revolves around famous personalities thanks to the publicity it generates, it becomes a cause for concern when it becomes damaging to a particular public figure. The research attempted to take a look at how much exposure people had to fake news about a particular celebrity. The findings:[17]

- The celebrity whose name was most associated with 'Fake News' was Tom Brady, an American football quarterback for the Tampa Bay Buccaneers of the National Football League. Between January and October 2022, 72,444,290 people mentioned 'fake news' along with his name. The stories ranged from his joining the American football team Miami Dolphins as a quarterback to his recent divorce announcement from the supermodel Gisele in 2022.
- Second place goes to Joseph James Rogan, an American UFC colour commentator, podcaster, comedian, actor and former television presenter, whose association with the phrase 'fake news' reached 39,276,532 people online. While doing his podcast with his guest Bryan 'Hotep Jesus' Sharpe, Joe Rogan mentioned that the Australian government is banning citizens from growing their own food, as they want to 'smoke out' anti-vaxxers. This news was fake and there was no such

law being proposed in Australia. Spotify paid $100m (£75m) in 2020 for rights to The Joe Rogan Experience, downloaded 200 million times a month. While Rogan's podcast has featured several notable guests who discuss various topics of interest, some episodes have featured false and misleading claims. Examples include baseless claims that the COVID-19 vaccine is a form of gene therapy that changes your DNA, that only ivermectin, an antiparasitic drug, can cure COVID, and that people who got the COVID-19 vaccine were at higher risk of contracting the virus as compared to unvaccinated people.[18]

- Elon Musk, founder of SpaceX and CEO of Tesla, was the third-ranked celebrity associated with the phrase 'fake news'. Even the Twitter boss himself faced a lot of scrutiny when a recent post of his with a doctored headline attributed to CNN was flagged by community notes as fake news. The community notes feature is available to Twitter users in the US and not in India. According to the Twitter help centre, 'Community Notes aim to create a better-informed world by empowering people on Twitter to collaboratively add context to potentially misleading Tweets. Contributors can leave notes on any Tweet and if enough contributors from different points of view rate that note as helpful, the note will be publicly shown on a Tweet'. In 2022, Elon Musk's association with the phrase 'fake news' reached 39,276,532 people online.

- The fourth on the list is Tom Holland, the Spider-Man star, who found himself the subject of a fake viral rumour which stated that he had passed away. The fake news was spread by an Instagram account with 186,000 followers which claimed that Spider-Man's Tom Hollard died after falling into a well and freezing to death. The post received 20K likes.

Not just Hollywood celebrities, but Indian celebrities too have been subjected to fake news attacks in recent times. Rumours went viral that Hrithik Roshan and his girlfriend Saba Azad had moved into a 100-crore apartment, and that Kareena Kapoor Khan was pregnant for the third time.[19]

#	CELEBRITY FAKE NEWS INDEX	
	Name	**Reach**
1	Tom Brady	7,24,44,290
2	Joe Rogan	3,92,76,532
3	Elon Musk	2,66,60,800
4	Tom Holland	81,00,678
5	Kanye West	65,09,040
6	Leonardo DiCaprio	39,60,573
7	Shakira	37,82,124
8	Will Smith	34,17,106
9	Rihanna	29,37,002
10	Taylor Swift	25,86,030
11	Snoop Dogg	24,49,406
12	Kim Kardashian	24,08,193
13	Pete Davidson	23,25,395

CELEBRITY FAKE NEWS INDEX		
#	Name	Reach
14	Johnny Depp	17,85,746
15	Lebron James	14,76,540
16	Beyonce	12,97,984
17	Justin Bieber	11,90,264
18	Amber Heard	9,77,366
19	Cardi B	8,21,794
20	Selena Gomez	7,27,891
*Based on the appearance of celebrity name alongside the phrase 'fake news'		

Source: 'Ranked: Celebrities Most Associated with Fake News', ExpressVPN[20]

Fake News: Culture Jamming the Brands

Are objective facts a thing of the past? In a *post-fact* world, objective facts are replaced by *alternative facts*. This means that we are living in a post-truth environment where objective facts have become irrelevant and emotional appeals are used to influence public opinion. So, can alternative facts be considered real facts? No, they are driven by intuition or feelings, regardless of truth.

The 'post-fact' world is swamped by messages which cannot be verified and lack objectivity. Both traditional and social media platforms are competing with one another to push the post-fact trend. This spells trouble for brands as fake news puts the brands at risk. The emergence of the 'misinformation age' can be said to be the troublesome child of the information age where personal biases overshadow objective truth, thus fuelling the spread of fake news.

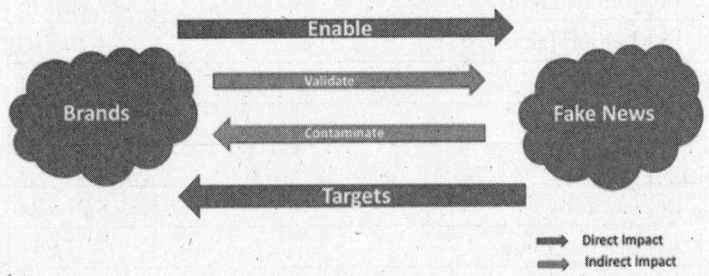

Source: 'How Truthiness, Fake News and Post-Fact Endanger Brands and What to Do about It'[21]

Fake News—A Double-Edged Sword for Brands

The trouble with brands is that they could either be the propagator or the victim of fake news. They may use fake news to their advantage and may also find themselves attacked by it. So, fake news can either tarnish a brand or end up being validated by one. In August 2017, Starbucks became the victim of fake news spread via social media. A fake advertisement falsely claimed that the coffee chain was offering a 40 per cent discount on their products to all illegal immigrants in America. Starbucks quickly shot down the rumours of the #BorderFreeCoffee brand promotion. The official Starbucks Twitter account put out a tweet saying, 'We're sorry but you've been misinformed,' and explained that the company was not sponsoring any such event. In order to combat the fake news, Starbucks began replying to each individual separately, refuting the advertisement.[22]

Source: Business Insider[23]

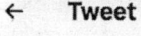

← **Tweet**

 **Starbucks Coffee** ✅   ...
@Starbucks

Replying to @Trumpservative

We're sorry but you've been misinformed. Starbucks
is not sponsoring any such event.

3:45 AM · Aug 5, 2017

13 Retweets   **2** Quote Tweets   **15** Likes

Source: Twitter, Starbucks Coffee[24]

In India, Kalyan Jewellers was the victim of a fake video
which claimed that the company sold impure gold. This

damaged the company's reputation and led to direct and indirect financial loss to the company worth INR 500 crore. This fake video culture jammed Kalyan Jewellers' claim of offering 100 per cent pure gold ornaments. Similarly, ITC's Aashirvaad brand of atta (wheat flour) was targeted by a fake video claiming that the product had plastic in it, resulting in a decline in sales across many states in the country. This advertisement culture jammed the company's claim of 'India's No. 1 Atta Brand'.[25]

With the power of social media as a source of information, and consumers' inability to distinguish between fake and real information, the reputation of a brand is always at stake. Not only can fake news damage the reputation of a brand, but it also affects its competitive advantage and the trust of its stakeholders. Brooke Binkoswki, editor of the fact-checking website Snopes. com, stated that 'fake news can hurt businesses financially while destroying trust and creating an atmosphere in which people don't know who they can trust'.[26]

Brands are vulnerable to fake news as consumers are unable or unwilling to identify false information. The consumer's cognitive bias makes them fall for fake stories and then motivates them to share it with their connections, friends and followers on social media. Looking at the source, these connections tend to believe that the fake stories are genuine and share them further, leading to the amplification of the fake news on social media.

Culture jammers use a variety of tactics to subvert and undermine the messages of corporate advertising, including parody, satire and guerrilla marketing. By taking the symbols and language of advertising and using them in unexpected ways, culture jammers seek to expose the hidden agendas of corporations and reveal the underlying social and political realities that are often obscured by the glossy veneer of advertising. One common tactic used by culture jammers is to create fake advertisements that mimic the style and tone of real ads, but with subversive messages that challenge consumer culture and promote alternative values. These ads can be disseminated through social media and other channels, reaching a wide audience and creating a buzz around the issues that the culture jammers are promoting.

Another tactic used by culture jammers is to hack into corporate websites and social media accounts, posting messages or images that contradict or satirize the company's official messaging. This can be a highly effective way of drawing attention to the discrepancies between a company's public image and its actual practices, and can create a groundswell of public opinion that can lead to real change.

In the year 2016 just before the US presidential election, PepsiCo shares dropped by 4 per cent owning to a fake news story about the beverage giant's then-CEO Indra Nooyi telling Donald Trump supporters to 'take their business elsewhere'. What had actually happened was that on 10 November 2016, while being interviewed at the *New York Times* Dealbook conference, Ms Nooyi stated that 'the process of democracy happened. We just need to let life go on.'[27] Picking a lead from this, the Conservative Treehouse blog spread the fake news with a sensational headline that said 'PepsiCo CEO Tells Trump Supporters to Take Their Business Elsewhere'. This was enough meat for social media to circulate this sensational news with the #boycottpepsi and #Pepsiboycott hashtags.

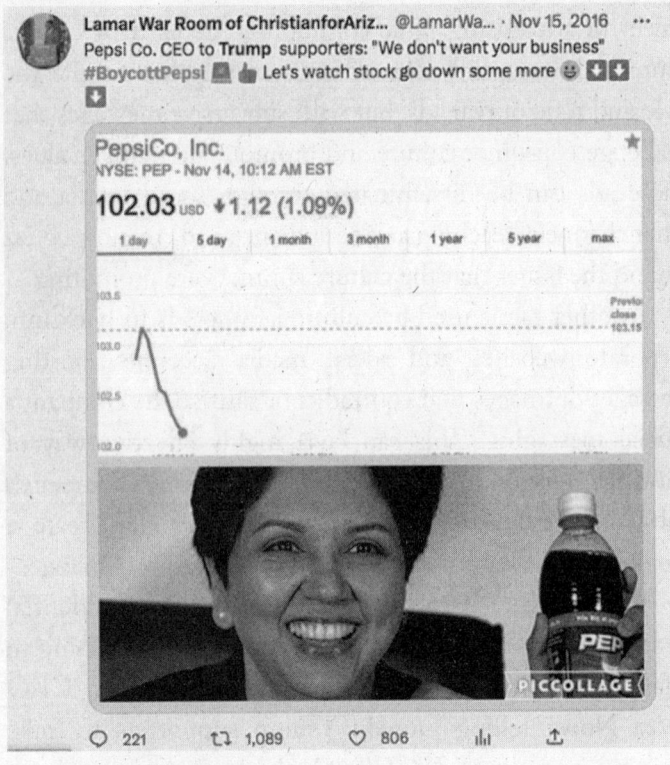

Source: Twitter[28]

Brands—Fake It to Make It

So, are brands victims or purveyors of fake news? This question needs extensive analysis of the purpose, reality and fictionalization of the brand communication. We understand that brands are under pressure to sell more and make profits. In the competitive market landscape, where supply often outstrips demand, brands are sometimes compelled to persuade consumers to buy more through misleading communication. Who would have known that pizza would be sold not based on its ingredients or service, but on 'bringing happiness to consumers'? Domino's Pizza's claim of '*Khushiyon ki* home delivery' (home delivery of happiness) is a claim that could be seen as fake, considering that pizza is junk food and can cause obesity. Similarly, leading beverage giant Coca-Cola claiming to bring 'happiness and peace' to its customers has become one of the main cultural purveyors of truthiness and post-fact.

Another brand advertising practice is using questions in the headline, like Domino's Pizza's 'Hungry Kya?' or Ford Motors' 'Have you driven a Ford lately?' or 'Did someone say McDonald's?' The use of questions in headlines can be best understood by Betteridge's Law. Originating from journalism, this law states that news outlets use question headlines for stories that lack sufficient facts to support the main point.[29] This can be applicable to advertising which asks questions in their headlines to which the answer is often 'no'. In such cases, the brand is making an impression which they cannot substantiate. These are just a few of many examples where brands have been purveyors of truthiness and post-fact.

While there are many examples of misleading brand communication, here are a few:

1. **Health claims:** Some brands make exaggerated health claims that are not backed up by scientific evidence. For example, a brand may claim that its product can cure a certain disease when there is no scientific proof to support that claim.

2. **Greenwashing:** This is when a company portrays itself as environmentally friendly or sustainable without actually making significant efforts to reduce its environmental impact. For example, a company might use eco-friendly packaging but still engage in practices that harm the environment.

3. **Hidden fees:** Some brands advertise a low price for a product or service but then tack on hidden fees that significantly increase the final cost. This can be misleading to consumers who think they are getting a good deal.

4. **False advertising:** This is when a brand makes false or misleading statements about its products or services. For example, a brand may claim that its product is made with all-natural ingredients when it actually contains synthetic chemicals.

5. **Deceptive labelling:** Some brands use misleading labelling to make their products seem healthier or more natural than they actually are. For example, a product may be labelled as 'low-fat' even though it is high in sugar or other unhealthy ingredients.

There have been many instances of brands making false health claims in their marketing and advertising materials. Here are a few examples:

1. In 2010, Coca-Cola was sued for falsely claiming that Vitaminwater could prevent eye disease, promote healthy joints and support the immune system. The company eventually settled for $1.26 million and agreed to change its labelling and advertising.[30]

2. In 2008, the makers of Airborne settled a class-action lawsuit for $23.3 million for making false claims that their product could prevent colds and boost the immune system.[31]

3. In 2010, the Federal Trade Commission charged POM Wonderful with making false claims that its pomegranate juice could prevent or treat heart disease, prostate cancer and other illnesses. The company eventually settled for $34 million.[32]

4. Patanjali, a popular Indian FMCG company, has faced criticism for allegedly making false claims about the health benefits of its products. For instance, the company claimed that its Coronil tablets could cure COVID-19, which led to a lot of controversy and backlash. The Indian government eventually asked Patanjali to stop advertising Coronil as a COVID-19 cure.[33]

5. Dabur, another Indian FMCG company, has faced criticism for making false health claims about its products. In 2016, the Advertising Standards Council of India (ASCI) found that Dabur's Chyawanprash ad claiming to boost immunity within five weeks was misleading and unsubstantiated.[34]

Fake News—Cultural Jamming the Socio-Cultural Dynamics

Fake news is dangerous when it comes to spreading misinformation and culture jamming the cultural and social popular beliefs of a nation's populations, especially in an age where information travels rapidly. Fighting fake news becomes difficult, as its impact can be felt at both the individual and societal levels. The exchange of information is vital to the social and cultural dynamics of any nation. Culture is nothing more than the collection of information acquired through social transmission, education, language and other means. However, not all information is true, leading to individuals living in doubt and struggling to adapt to their cultural and social environment. Religion is an integral part of culture and cultural values form the foundation of religious beliefs. Religion can be seen as a subset of culture and an expression of spirituality.

Fake news has not spared religious beliefs, eroding the foundation of culture through the spread of misinformation. Early Christian theories have been fogged by sensational and captivating claims that Jesus married Mary Magdalene, the woman who travelled with Jesus and was witness to his crucifixion. Though this story is fake, with there being no evidence of their marriage, it keeps on surfacing time and time again. This narrative gained attention through Dan Brown's best-selling fictional novel 'The Da Vinci Code' in 2003, where he presented the idea of their marriage and the church's efforts to conceal it for centuries.

In a recent controversy, Prime Minister of Nepal K.P. Oli alleged that India stole Nepal's cultural fact, claiming that Ayodhya, the birthplace of Lord Rama, is located in Nepal and that Lord Rama was Nepali and not Indian. 'How did residents of Ayodhya, which India claims is in Uttar Pradesh, come to Janakpur to marry Sita? There were no phones at that time, so how did they communicate? During those times, marriages were arranged in nearby kingdoms only. No one used to travel so far to marry,' Oli had remarked.

Another controversy surrounding Lord Rama arose when K.S. Bhagwan, a Kannada professor and writer, made an unverified statement that according to the Valmiki Ramayana, Lord Rama used to drink wine every afternoon with his wife Sita. Such unverified statements are dangerous for the culture or society at large as they influence the religious faith of people and hurt their religious and cultural sentiments.[35]

Fake News—Culture-Jamming Scientific Discoveries

WhatsApp, the popular messaging service, is one of the biggest platforms responsible for the spread of fake news. People can not only share messages with individuals but can also post them in groups or broadcast them to their connections. Globally, WhatsApp has over 2.26 billion unique users, with nearly 100 billion messages being shared every day.[36] India has the highest number of WhatsApp users at around 400 million and including the US and

Brazil, it accounts for 573 million. With such a large base, it has become a preferred platform for the dissemination of fake news.

One of the ways fake news is spread on WhatsApp is to promote religious mythical events as precursors to modern scientific discoveries. These fake messages with deliberately exaggerated headlines are formatted to look like authentic news reports. While Facebook played a key role in spreading fake news in the US to influence voting patterns, WhatsApp has become the preferred platform for the dissemination of fake news in India.

One such outrageous claim was that cow urine cures cancer and coronavirus. Biotechnology scientists at Junagadh Agriculture University claimed that after years of research, they have discovered that cow urine can cure cancer. They compared cow urine with chemotherapy and claimed that while chemotherapy killed off both cancer cells and healthy cells, cow urine killed only cancer cells.[37] The belief in Hindu culture that cow urine is pure contributed to the promotion of this non-scientific theory. This claim spread like wildfire on social media, and in no time, bottles containing cow urine began to be sold in retail outlets.

While cow urine contains some minerals like sodium, potassium, creatinine, phosphorus and epithelial cells, it still does not cure cancer as claimed.

Another instance involves a Union Minister advising Indian Institute of Technology (IIT) students to learn technology from the mystical 'Pushpaka Vimana' flying chariot, which is mentioned in the Ramayana. He also went on to recommend the inclusion of Hindu mythologies and Vedic texts in IIT's curriculum. Fake news creators projected the Pushpaka Vimana as a precursor to the Wright Brothers' aeroplane design.[38] Photoshopped images of flying chariots began spreading on social media, with intrepid users calculating the distance from Ayodhya in India to Sri Lanka, and estimating the duration of the flight. The dissemination of such fake news led to debates on social media and polarizing opinions on the legitimacy of these claims.

The emergence of fake news as a tool for culture jamming is posing a threat to harmony both in India and globally. Though efforts are being made by social media platforms to combat fake news, the presence of clickbait headlines, animated graphics, fake videos, unverified stories and facts amplified through social media platforms remains a challenge and can have a harmful impact on people, brands and the nation as a whole.

III

How Fake News Affects What We Buy and Consume

'A lie gets halfway around the world before the truth has a chance to get its pants on.'

—Winston Churchill

Fake news can have a significant impact on consumer behaviour. It can influence people's opinions, beliefs and purchasing decisions by presenting false or misleading information. When consumers start believing fake news, they may make decisions based on incorrect information, leading to unintended consequences. For example, if fake news reports claim that a certain product is harmful, consumers may avoid purchasing it, even if it happens to be safe and reliable. This can lead to a loss of sales and revenue for the affected companies, and can even tarnish the reputation of the product and the industry. On the other hand, fake news can also create a false sense of demand for a product, leading to overproduction and waste. Thus, fake news can cause significant harm to both consumers and businesses.

Fake news can affect what we buy and consume by spreading false information about products, services and companies. This misinformation can create unrealistic expectations, alter consumer preferences and even result in dangerous purchasing decisions. For example, if a fake news article claims that a certain food product is harmful, people may stop buying it, even if the claim is not supported by scientific evidence. It is pertinent to cite the Maggi case here to substantiate how fake news can damage a brand's reputation. The claim that Maggi noodles contained lead beyond permissible limits was found to be false as scientific tests conducted by the FDA showed no dangerous levels of lead in the noodles.[1] However, this fake news had already dealt a severe blow to Maggi's reputation across the world and, as a result, it was banned in many countries. On the other hand, if a fake news article promotes a product as a cure-all solution, people may purchase it without fully understanding its limitations or potential side effects. In both cases, fake news can distort the market and lead to unintended consequences.

There are many examples of fake news impacting consumer choice:

1. **Misleading product reviews:** Fake reviews can be created to make a product appear better than it is,

leading consumers to purchase a product that may not meet their expectations.

2. **False advertising claims:** Companies may spread false information about their products, such as false health claims, to entice consumers to purchase them.

3. **Disinformation campaigns:** Disinformation campaigns can be used to spread false information about a particular product, company or industry to sway consumer opinion and choices.

4. **Fabricated news articles:** Fake news articles can be created and spread through social media to discredit a particular product, company or industry.

These examples demonstrate how fake news can significantly impact consumer choice and behaviour, and it is important for consumers to be able to differentiate between credible sources of information and misinformation.

Do Colas Have Pesticides, and Can They Be Used as Toilet Cleaners?

Let us analyse the controversy that surrounded the cola giants like Pepsi and Coca-Cola. Over the years, these two companies have faced the following fake allegations:

- These drinks have chemicals which can be used to clean toilets
- They contain harmful levels of pesticide

- Farmers in India are using colas as a pesticide for their crops

The first claim that Coca-Cola can be used as a toilet cleaner is false. Coca-Cola, or any sugary beverages for that matter, should not be used as toilet cleaners or for any cleaning purposes. These drinks contain high levels of sugar and acid which can cause damage to surfaces and are not effective cleaners. Additionally, the use of soft drinks for cleaning can pose a health risk as the combination of chemicals can produce toxic fumes. It is always better to use products that are specifically designed for cleaning purposes.

Indian yoga guru Baba Ramdev told news agency IANS that people should drink hot water, milk or traditional Indian juice and practise yoga early in the morning instead of consuming soft drinks.[2] 'Cold drinks have no place in our society, they are basically toilet cleaners,' he said, suggesting that people should abandon Western fast food and cold drink culture. Baba Ramdev laid the foundations of his ayurvedic and herbal range of products under the Patanjali brand, which he established as a response to foreign brands, riding on the wave of nationalism.

The second claim that cola drinks contain pesticides is false. Cola drinks are made from water, sugar, flavourings and carbonation. There is no evidence to suggest that pesticides are added to the drinks. However, it is important to note that some ingredients used to make cola drinks, such as high fructose corn syrup, may be derived from crops that have been treated with pesticides. It is recommended to thoroughly wash and peel fruits and vegetables before consuming them to minimize the risk of consuming any pesticide residue. This fake news that Coca-Cola has pesticides in it led to a drop in the beverage's sales in the third quarter of 2003 by 11 per cent. This is the first instance where the cola giant declared the damage caused by reported allegations by the Delhi-based Centre for Science and Environment (CSE), mentioning that the soft drink brands of PepsiCo and Coca-Cola contained pesticides and insecticides beyond the limits set by the European Economic Commission (EEC).[3]

The third claim that farmers in India are using carbonated drinks like Coca-Cola, Pepsi and Thums Up as pesticides is also false. The fake news reports that make this claim suggest that the farmers do so as the carbonated drinks are cheaper than actual chemical-based pesticides. This is pertinently false as cola drinks are ineffective as pesticides. Pesticides are chemicals designed to kill or control pests such as insects, weeds and fungi, whereas cola drinks primarily contain sugar and caffeine, which are not toxic to pests and will not control or kill them. Additionally, using cola drinks as pesticides could be harmful to the environment and non-target species. It is recommended to use registered and appropriate pesticides for pest control.

Many brands fall prey to the 'Fake News Effect', which refers to the negative impact that false or misleading information can have on consumer behaviour and attitudes towards brands. When consumers encounter fake news or misinformation about a brand, it can shape their opinions or beliefs about the brand, negatively influencing their purchasing intentions or decisions. This effect can be particularly damaging for brands that are already facing challenges or negative perceptions, as the spread of false information can exacerbate existing problems and create new ones. Brands can mitigate the impact of fake news by engaging in active reputation management, regularly monitoring the spread of false information and responding promptly and transparently to any misinformation that arises. Though fake news has been studied in detail in the context of politics, it is also true that fake news can impact people's attitudes and behaviours of consumers. It can influence consumer brand perception and intention to buy. Therefore, the nature (fake vs. real) and valence (+ve vs -ve) affect consumer buying behaviour.

Does Kurkure Contain Plastic?

There were many fake claims surrounding Kurkure, the PepsiCo-owned corn-based snack, that it contained plastic and that people could verify this claim for themselves by setting the snack on fire. While Kurkure, a snack made from cornmeal, spices and edible oils, did not contain any plastic, the nature of these claims led to a lot of people believing in them, resulting in a toll on the reputation of the brand even as the fake claims were debunked by independent lab tests and by PepsiCo, which repeatedly asserted that the snack was fit for consumption and did not contain plastic. The fake claims repeatedly mentioned how Kurkure would melt like plastic when set alight, but the reality was that Kurkure, like any other salty snack, would melt upon being set alight not because of plastic in it but because of carbohydrates and dry starch. Customers, however, became jittery, resulting in PepsiCo filing a case in Delhi High Court in 2018 against Facebook, Twitter and YouTube, with the court ordering the removal of URLs and links spreading this fake news. The High Court on 1 June 2018 ordered the removal of 3412 Facebook links, 20,244 Facebook posts, 242 YouTube videos, six Instagram links and 562 tweets pertaining to the spread of this fake news. PepsiCo claimed that it was their deliberate effort to fight fake news attacking its brand, and took proactive steps to build trust in its brand by inviting people to visit their factories and witness the manufacturing process of Kurkure. Further, they issued disclaimers and public notices in the mainstream as well as social media outlets disclosing the ingredients that are used in the manufacturing of Kurkure.[4]

Misleading or Fake Product Reviews

The internet has transformed how consumers buy and shop online. They are more than motivated to look for other people's experiences and reviews of the product they intend to purchase. Online reviews can have a significant impact on buying behaviour as they provide potential customers with information about a product or service from other consumers. Positive reviews can build trust and credibility for a brand, increasing the likelihood that a customer will make a purchase. Conversely, negative reviews can discourage customers from making a purchase or prompt them to look for alternative options. Additionally, online reviews can provide customers with valuable information such as product features, performance and overall satisfaction, which can help them make informed buying decisions. In conclusion, online reviews play an important role in shaping consumer perception and decision-making, and can greatly influence buying behaviour. Fake reviews can have a significant impact on buying behaviour. They can influence a consumer's perception of a product and skew their decision-making process. When fake positive reviews are present, consumers may have unrealistic expectations and be disappointed with their purchase. On the other hand, fake negative reviews can falsely steer potential customers away from a good product. In both cases, fake reviews can lead to a loss of trust in online reviews and damage the reputation of the product or the reviewing platform. It is important for consumers to be able to distinguish between real and fake reviews in order to make informed purchasing decisions.

There are several types of fake online reviews, including:

1. **Paid reviews:** These are reviews that are written by individuals who have been paid to write a positive review for a particular product or service.
2. **Competitor reviews:** These are fake reviews written by individuals who are associated with a competitor of the product or service being reviewed. They may write

fake negative reviews in an attempt to damage the reputation of the product or service.

3. **Incentivized reviews:** These are reviews written by individuals who have received some type of incentive, such as a discount or free product, in exchange for writing a review.

4. **Fabricated reviews:** These are reviews that are completely made up and contain false information.

5. **Review farming:** This is the practice of creating fake profiles and using them to write fake reviews. The fake profiles are often used to write both positive and negative reviews in an attempt to manipulate the reputation of a product or service.

6. **Sockpuppet reviews:** An individual may create fake accounts to write multiple positive or negative reviews for a particular brand or business.

It is important to be aware of such fake online reviews and to exercise caution when making decisions based on online reviews. There have been numerous cases of online scammers forcing restaurants in New York to give them gift certificates under the threat of negative reviews. In Chicago and San Francisco, a well-planned digital crime targeted a vegan restaurant with a slew of one-star reviews, subsequently blackmailing it for money.[5] This trend is dangerous as the businesses are highly vulnerable to such blackmails where the restaurant's reputation relies on the 'wisdom of the crowd' because people may only choose to go there after checking out online reviews as to learn how the community rates the product or services of the brand or business.

Attention-Based vs Creator-Led Economy[6]

We are moving from an attention-based to a creator-led economy. An attention-based economy refers to a theoretical economic system in which the value of goods, services and digital assets is determined based on the amount of attention they receive. This concept has gained increasing popularity in the digital age, where attention is a scarce resource and a valuable commodity. In an attention-based economy, attention is seen as a finite resource that individuals and businesses can compete for. The more attention a particular item receives, the more valuable it becomes. For example, a social media post that generates a large number of likes, comments and shares is considered more valuable than a post that receives little engagement. This type of economy is relevant to the digital world, where there is a growing demand for attention from individuals and businesses alike. Companies compete for attention by creating engaging content, offering free services and leveraging social media and other digital platforms to reach a larger audience. However, some experts have expressed concerns about the potential negative impacts of an attention-based economy. These include the risk of promoting shallow and sensational content over more meaningful and educational content, and the potential for increased competition for attention to lead to the exploitation of users' personal data.

Despite these concerns, the attention-based economy is likely to play an increasingly important role in the digital world in the coming years.

Businesses all around the world compete to appear on the first page of Google's search results in order to gain the attention of online users searching for a particular keyword. A user's review or feedback is a key component influencing the ranking page search algorithms. In this context, fake reviews are a form of manipulation designed to capture people's attention and influence their opinions, behaviour and purchasing decisions. Fake reviews are often created with the intention of promoting a product or service and can be used to boost their reputation, attract more customers or deceive people into believing they are of higher quality than they actually are. By generating buzz and creating a false sense of demand, fake reviews help businesses reap economic benefits from consumer attention. However, fake reviews can also harm the credibility of online platforms and erode consumer trust, which is why many companies and organizations are taking steps to identify and eliminate fake reviews from their sites.

On the other hand, the term 'creator economy' generally refers to the trend of content creation and monetization through platforms that allow individuals to share their creations with a large audience. This can encompass a wide range of content, including written articles, videos, music, photography and more. Some popular examples of platforms that facilitate the creator economy include YouTube, Twitch, TikTok, Substack and Patreon. These platforms provide a space for creators to share their work and connect with fans, while also offering various tools and features to help creators monetize their content. This can include advertising revenue, subscription services and crowdfunding campaigns.

The creator economy has opened up new opportunities for individuals to earn income through their talents and creativity, and has also created a new landscape for businesses to connect with audiences and customers. The growth of the creator economy is seen as a reflection of the increasing importance of digital media and the trend towards decentralization of the traditional media landscape.

Fake reviews can also have a significant impact on the creator economy, as they can manipulate the perceived popularity and quality of products and services. This can lead to unfair competition and harm to honest businesses, while also undermining consumer trust in online reviews and recommendations. In the creator economy, fake reviews can be used to artificially inflate the popularity and success of certain creators, leading to unequal distribution of opportunities and income. This can also make it more difficult for new and genuine creators to gain recognition and succeed in the industry.

To combat the effects of fake reviews, platforms and marketplaces can implement various measures such as reviewing and verifying the authenticity of reviews, using machine learning algorithms to detect suspicious patterns of activity and allowing consumers to report and flag fake reviews. However, these measures can be expensive and time-consuming to implement and maintain, and they may not always be fully effective in detecting and removing all fake reviews. As such, it remains important for consumers to be vigilant and critical when evaluating online reviews and recommendations, and to look for signs of fake or biased reviews.

According to some surveys, a significant percentage of people rely on online reviews when making purchase decisions. The exact percentage can vary depending on the type of product or service being considered, as well as the age and demographic of the individual. However, some estimates suggest that anywhere from 60 to 90 per cent of consumers consult online reviews before making a purchase. For example, a survey by Vendasta found that 92 per cent of consumers read online reviews for purchasing, while 40 per cent of consumers form an opinion after reading one to three reviews. Star ratings are crucial for the evaluation of a business, with a higher rating of four to five stars holding greater weight.[7] This highlights the growing importance of online reviews in today's marketplace and the need for businesses to carefully manage their online reputation.

Are Paid Reviews Illegal?

Paid reviews are not necessarily illegal but they can be considered deceptive or fraudulent if they are not disclosed as paid. In many countries, including the United States, it is illegal to engage in false advertising, which can include posting fake reviews or failing to disclose that a review is paid. Additionally, many platforms have policies that prohibit the posting of paid reviews without disclosure, and failure to comply with these policies can result in penalties or account suspension.

TripAdvisor, one of the largest user-generated content online travel platforms, was the first in 2015 to unmask the company Promo Salento for posting paid reviews for hospitality businesses in Italy.[8] The investigation began when affected business owners contacted TripAdvisor and shared the letters received from Promo Salento offering to write online reviews to boost the business profile of their companies on TripAdvisor. An agitation led by Observer restaurant critic Jay Rayner backed by many affected restaurant owners took the matter to TripAdvisor to curb the practice of fake reviews on its site and take action against the culprits. With over one billion reviews on the website, a Twitter hashtag campaign #noreceiptnoreview was launched to compel the website to only publish reviews which were accompanied by a receipt. 'TripAdvisor have admitted they have a problem with fake reviews, and if you have a business model that functions on trust, then you need to do something to protect that,' said Rayner. 'At the moment, I only use TripAdvisor to get a list of places in a particular town I'm going to—I ignore the rankings.'[9] Though TripAdvisor has a long list of review guidelines for users, it still does not ensure that the account holder posting a review has evidence to show that they used the service. The guidelines cover that the review should be first-hand information or experience, relevant to trip experience, unique and recent experience, unbiased and nonmanipulative. Paid reviews, review exchanges, incentives for review and review gating are also prohibited.

In 2019, TripAdvisor was the first review platform to table a transparency report stating the steps it took to fight fake reviews. In 2021, about 3.6 per cent of the reviews posted on the platform were fraudulent. Out of those, TripAdvisor managed to prevent 67.1 per cent of the fake reviews from ever appearing on the platform.[10]

When the basis of a website is customer trust, it becomes essential for that company to adjust its scoring algorithms in such a way that it does not allow fake or paid reviews to influence consumer choice or preference. So, the outcome was that the TripAdvisor fake reviewer—the owner of Promo Salento—was imprisoned for nine months and fined €8,000. This was one of the first landmark judgments by the Italian government in the history of paid fake reviews. Harvard Business School Professor Michael Luka published a paper titled 'Reviews, Reputation and Revenue: The Case of Yelp.com' analysing Yelp's rating model of restaurants and the impact on demand.[11] His research findings showed:

1. A one-star increase in a Yelp rating leads to a 5–9 per cent increase in revenue.
2. This effect is driven by independent restaurants; ratings do not affect restaurants with chain affiliation.
3. The market share of chain restaurants has declined as Yelp penetration has increased.

4. Consumers do not use all available information and are more responsive to quality changes that are more visible.
5. Consumers respond more strongly when a rating contains more information.

In 2021, almost 20 per cent of reviews did not clear Yelp's verification process and were categorized as 'not recommended', appearing at the bottom of Yelp's pages. Other companies like Amazon, who are also concerned with paid fake reviews, sued 1114 unidentified people for charging money as low as $5 to post reviews on 'Fiverr'—a global online freelance services marketplace. Amazon also has review guidelines on their website stating:[12]

The following are types of reviews that they do not allow:

- A review by someone who has a direct or indirect financial interest in the product.
- A review by someone perceived to have a close personal relationship with the product's owner, author or artist.
- A review by the product manufacturer, posing as an unbiased shopper.
- Multiple negative reviews for the same product from one customer.
- A review in exchange for a monetary reward.
- A review of a game in exchange for bonus in-game credits.
- A negative review from a seller on a competitor's product.

- A positive review from an artist on a peer's album in exchange for a similar favour.

In many cases, when a review is rejected, the customer is sometimes unclear about the reason. If an employee from the same organization buys the author's book, their review may be rejected as Amazon may consider them biased due to close association.

Website review guidelines aim to ensure that reviews on a website are genuine and trustworthy while preventing the posting of fake reviews. However, these guidelines are not foolproof and there is always a risk of fake reviews slipping through. To help prevent fake reviews, website review guidelines typically require that reviews be written by real customers who have actually used the product or service being reviewed. Guidelines may also prohibit reviews that are fraudulent, misleading or those that violate the website's terms of service. Some websites also use automated systems or manual moderators to screen reviews and identify potential fake reviews. For example, they may use algorithms to detect patterns of suspicious behaviour, such as a large number of reviews from the same IP address, or reviews that use identical language.

Despite these stringent measures, some fake reviews may still go undetected. This is why it is important for consumers to approach online reviews with a critical eye, and to consider multiple sources of information before making a purchasing decision. It's also a good idea to look for reviews from verified buyers or to consult with friends, family, or other trusted sources before making a purchase based on online reviews. In India, the government, under the Bureau of Indian Standards (BIS), has set up a new standard called IS 19000:2022. Its objective is to certify the process related to the collection, moderation and publication of online reviews. Some of the guidelines of these new standards are that online reviews cannot be edited after publishing, no foul language is permitted, and those who have submitted fake reviews are prohibited from doing so in the future and so on. Many big e-commerce retailers were part of this committee including Zomato, Swiggy, Meta, Amazon, Tata Sons and Reliance to name a few.

All That Glitters Is Not Gold

Advertising serves as a reason for consumers to buy the product, but there is a difference between making true and false claims. We know that consumers buy brands because of rational or emotional reasons. False advertising claims can have a significant impact on buyer behaviour, as they can result in erosion of trust in a particular brand or product. When a consumer discovers that a product or service has been falsely advertised, they may feel misled and deceived, which can lead to a loss of confidence in the brand.

As a result, consumers may be less likely to purchase products from the brand in the future, which can have a negative impact on the brand's reputation and sales. In some cases, false advertising claims can also lead to legal action, which can further damage a brand's reputation and credibility.

Additionally, false advertising claims can have broader implications for consumer behaviour, as they can lead to a lack of trust in advertising and marketing in general. This can make it more difficult for other brands to effectively promote their products and services to consumers.

Overall, false advertising claims can have a significant impact on buyer behaviour, both in terms of their relationship with a specific brand and their overall attitudes towards advertising and marketing. It is therefore important for brands to be transparent and truthful in their advertising and marketing efforts to maintain the trust and confidence of their customers.

False advertising claims can take various forms, but some of the most common types include:

1. **False statements about a product's performance:** This includes claims that a product can do something it cannot, such as promising weight loss without exercise or diet changes.
2. **False claims about a product's ingredients:** This includes claims that a product contains ingredients that it does not, or that the ingredients are more effective or have more benefits than they actually do.
3. **Misleading statements about a product's price or value:** This includes false sales or discount claims, or inflated price comparisons with other products.

4. **Deceptive endorsements or testimonials:** This includes using fake or misleading endorsements or testimonials from celebrities, experts or satisfied customers to promote a product.

5. **False claims about a product's safety or health benefits:** This includes claims that a product is safe for use when it is not, or that it can cure or prevent a serious medical condition without scientific evidence.

6. **Misleading comparisons with other products:** This includes the use of false or deceptive comparisons with other products, such as claiming that a product is 'better than the leading brand' without providing evidence to support the claim.

7. **False claims about a product's environmental impact:** This includes making false or exaggerated claims about a product's eco-friendliness or environmental impact, such as claiming that a product is biodegradable when it is not.

False Advertising Scandals[13]

Volkswagen's 'Clean Diesel'

In March 2016, the Federal Trade Commission (FTC) charged Volkswagen Group of America Inc. for running a misleading advertisement campaign called Clean Diesel. This campaign falsely claimed that Volkswagen's diesel engines were environmentally friendly. The Volkswagen emissions scandal, also known as 'Dieselgate', is a notorious case involving Volkswagen Group's cheating on emissions tests for diesel-powered vehicles in the United States and other countries.

In September 2015, the United States Environmental Protection Agency (EPA) issued a notice of violation of the Clean Air Act to Volkswagen, alleging that the company had installed software in diesel engines that enabled them to cheat on emissions tests. This software allowed the engines to detect when they were being tested and to temporarily reduce emissions of nitrogen oxides (NOx) to comply with regulations. During normal driving, however, the vehicles emitted up to forty times more NOx than allowed by law.

The scandal resulted in the recall of millions of Volkswagen, Audi and Porsche vehicles worldwide, as well as fines and settlements totalling billions of dollars. It also led to criminal charges against Volkswagen executives, including the CEO at the time, and sparked a wider investigation into diesel emissions in Europe. The case highlighted the importance of independent regulatory oversight and the need for companies to take responsibility for their actions. It also underscored the challenges of regulating complex technologies and the importance of transparency in the automotive industry. FTC alleges that from 2015 to 2021 Volkswagen deceived consumers by marketing and advertising around 550,000 diesel fuel cars by claiming that these cars were low-emission, environmentally friendly and compliant with emissions standards.

Red Bull Gives You Wings

Red Bull was sued in 2014 over its marketing slogan 'Red Bull Gives You Wings'. The lawsuit was filed in the United States by a group of consumers who alleged that the advertising was deceptive and that they had been misled into believing that the energy drink would provide them with enhanced physical and mental performance.

The plaintiffs argued that the advertising slogan was false and misleading, and that Red Bull had engaged in false advertising and unjust enrichment. They also argued that the company had failed to disclose the true nature of the product's ingredients and the potential health risks associated with its consumption.

In response to the lawsuit, Red Bull agreed to pay out $13 million to settle the claims. As part of the settlement, the company did not admit any wrongdoing but agreed to modify its marketing and advertising practices, including its slogan.

New Balance's 'hidden beauty secret'

In 2011, New Balance released a new toning and walking shoe which included a technology called 'hidden board' that claimed it could help wearers burn more calories by increasing muscle activation in the legs. However, it is important to note that there is currently limited scientific evidence to support the claim that this shoe, or any other shoe, can significantly increase calorie burn. While certain types of shoes can change the way your body moves and potentially increase muscle activation in some areas, the actual increase in calorie burn is likely to be small and will depend on many factors, including individual physiology, intensity of exercise, diet and sleep.

So, while the New Balance shoe may offer some benefits for certain types of exercise, it is unlikely to be a magic solution for weight loss or calorie burning. As with any exercise programme, it is important to focus on overall health and fitness, including regular exercise, a healthy diet, and adequate rest and recovery.

Three women filed a claim against the shoe brand asserting that it did not help them lose weight. The court ordered New Balance to pay the plaintiffs $2.3 million to resolve the case. New Balance claimed that their shoe was toned in such a way that it would make the wearer feel they were running on sand, with the design making it hard to stay balanced, which would result in an extra calorie burn of 8 per cent compared to regular shoes. They referred to this as a 'hidden beauty secret'.

Hyundai and Kia—Falsely Advertised Fuel Efficiency

In 2020, Hyundai and Kia agreed to pay a $210 million civil penalty to the US government to settle claims that they over-advertised the fuel efficiency of their vehicles. In November 2021, a lawsuit was filed against Hyundai and Kia in the US District Court for the Central District of California, alleging that the companies over-advertised the horsepower of certain vehicles. The lawsuit claims that the automakers used deceptive marketing to exaggerate the horsepower ratings of their cars and that this misrepresentation led consumers to pay more for vehicles that did not actually meet the advertised horsepower levels. The lawsuit specifically names the Hyundai Veloster N, Elantra N and Sonata N-Line, as well as the Kia Stinger, K5 GT and Forte GT. The plaintiffs in the case are seeking damages for the alleged misrepresentation.

It is worth noting that while automakers do sometimes use 'optimistic' testing conditions to generate horsepower ratings, there is a regulatory framework in place to ensure that advertised horsepower figures are based on standardized testing procedures. If the lawsuit against Hyundai and Kia is successful, it could indicate that the automakers violated these regulations in their advertising practices. In another case in 2004, Hyundai paid around $85 million when it overstated the horsepower of the cars imported to the United States.

Taller, Stronger and Sharper

In India, there have been cases where face creams claim to provide fairer skin after regular use, cola drinks claim to provide instant energy and shampoo brands claim to stop hair fall or dandruff after just one wash.

Horlicks is a popular brand of malted milk drink that has been marketed as a health drink for many years. While it is true that Horlicks contains a variety of vitamins and minerals that can be beneficial to a child's health, the claim that it is clinically proven to make kids taller, stronger and sharper is not entirely accurate. There have been some studies that have shown a correlation between the consumption of Horlicks and improved growth in children. However, these studies are typically funded by the manufacturer and may not be entirely unbiased.[14] Additionally, the improvements observed are generally modest and can be attributed to the general nutritional benefits of the drink rather than any specific ingredients. Furthermore, the claim that Horlicks can make kids stronger and sharper is not supported by any scientific evidence. While proper nutrition is important for cognitive and physical development, there is no evidence to suggest that Horlicks is any better at providing these benefits than other sources of nutrition.

In summary, while Horlicks can be a healthy addition to a child's diet, the claim that it is clinically proven to make kids taller, stronger and sharper is not entirely accurate and should be taken with a grain of salt.

What Should Advertisers Do?

False advertising refers to the practice of making misleading or deceptive claims about a product or service in order to persuade consumers to purchase it. False advertising is illegal in many countries, including the US, and there are several guidelines that advertisers must follow to avoid making false claims. Here are some key guidelines for advertisers:

1. **Claims must be truthful:** Advertisers must ensure that all claims made in their advertisements are truthful and accurate. They must be able to substantiate any claims they make with scientific evidence, if necessary.

2. **Claims must not be misleading:** Advertisers must not use language or images that could mislead consumers. For example, an advertiser cannot claim that a product is 'all-natural' if it contains synthetic ingredients.

3. **Claims must be substantiated:** Advertisers must be able to support any claims they make with evidence, including scientific studies or customer reviews. They should not make claims that cannot be proven.

4. **Disclosures must be clear and conspicuous:** If an advertisement includes disclosures, such as information about the side effects of a medication, these disclosures must be clearly and conspicuously displayed.

5. **Comparative claims must be truthful and verifiable**: Advertisers can make comparative claims, such as claiming that their product is better than a competitor's product. However, these claims must be truthful and verifiable.

6. **Advertisers must not use deceptive imagery:** Advertisers must not use imagery that is deceptive or could mislead consumers. For example, an advertiser cannot use photos of a product that have been altered to make them appear larger or more effective than they really are.

7. **Advertisers must not use false testimonials:** Advertisers must not use false testimonials or

endorsements. They must be able to prove that any testimonials they use are from real customers who have used their product or service.

By following these guidelines, advertisers can help ensure that their advertisements are truthful and accurate and that consumers are not misled by false claims.

What Can Consumers Do?

If you believe that you have been a victim of false advertising, there are several steps you can take to address the issue:

1. **Gather evidence:** Collect any information that supports your claim of false advertising, such as print or digital advertisements, promotional materials, product packaging and receipts.
2. **Contact the company:** Contact the company that made the false advertising claim and explain your concerns. They may offer a resolution, such as a refund or an exchange.
3. **File a complaint:** If the company does not resolve your issue, you can file a complaint with the relevant regulatory agency, such as the Federal Trade Commission (FTC) in the US, which investigates false advertising claims.
4. **Seek legal assistance:** If you have suffered significant financial harm as a result of false advertising, you

may want to consider hiring a lawyer to help you seek compensation through legal action.

It is important to note that false advertising is illegal and can have serious consequences for companies that engage in it, including fines and damage to their reputation. By taking action, you are not only advocating for your own rights as a consumer, but you may also be helping others from falling victim to false advertising.

IV

Psychology of Fake News: Why Do People Fall For Fake News?

'If there's something you really want to believe, that's what you should question the most.'

—Penn Jillette

History is full of instances where deception has been used as a powerful strategy, from ancient tales like Helen of Troy to epics like the Ramayana or the Mahabharata. Fake news is a modern version of this strategy but what has changed is the ability to amplify fake news and spread it to a large audience with the help of social media. The psychology of fake news involves understanding how and why people consume, share and believe false information. Several factors can influence people's susceptibility to fake news, including cognitive biases, social influence and emotional responses.

Cognitive biases are mental shortcuts that can lead people to make errors in judgment and decision-making. For example, confirmation bias—the tendency to search for, interpret and remember information that confirms pre-existing beliefs—can make people more likely to believe and share fake news that aligns with their existing views. Cognitive biases can play a significant role in the spread and consumption of fake news. Here are a few ways in which cognitive biases can contribute to the proliferation of fake news:

Confirmation bias: This is the tendency to seek out and interpret information in a way that confirms our pre-existing beliefs. When people encounter news that supports their world view, they are more likely to believe it and share it, even if it is false. For example, if Rohan believes that higher education does not guarantee employability, then he might interpret news of a higher unemployment rate as supporting his belief. On the other hand, if Dolly believes that higher education guarantees employability, she might interpret the same news in a way that does not support her belief. Similarly, a person supporting a right-wing political party may prefer watching television channels that have a right-wing bias. Regarding medical bias, people who believe that COVID-19 vaccines are harmful will actively seek out information that supports their view and ignore any evidence to the contrary.

Confirmation bias prevents us from evaluating a situation objectively and can influence our choices without any objective factual information. In India, there have been many false claims about the origins of COVID-19, such as the virus being created in a Chinese lab or that it was intentionally spread by the Chinese government. These claims have been spread due to a confirmation bias among those who hold negative views of China. Similar rumours were spread regarding the COVID-19 vaccine, such that it contains cow urine or that it causes infertility. These rumours were spread due to a confirmation bias among those sceptical of the vaccine.

It is important to be aware of confirmation bias when consuming and sharing news, and to try to seek out information from a variety of sources. Fact-checking websites such as Alt News and BoomLive can be helpful in identifying and debunking fake news.

Availability heuristic: The availability heuristic is a cognitive bias in which people tend to rely on readily available information or examples when making decisions or judgements. This means that if something is more easily recalled, it may be considered as more important, relevant or probable. Fake news can exploit the availability heuristic by presenting false or misleading information in a way that is more memorable or sensational than accurate news. This can lead people to overestimate the frequency or likelihood of events that are actually rare or unlikely. For example, if a fake news story about a crime is widely circulated, people may be more likely to believe that crime rates are rising, even if they are not. In addition to exploiting the availability heuristic, fake news can also be spread through other cognitive biases such as confirmation bias (as mentioned earlier, the tendency to seek out information that confirms one's existing beliefs) and the illusory truth effect (the tendency to believe information that is repeated often). It is important for individuals to be aware of these biases and to critically evaluate the information they receive, especially in the age of social media where fake news can spread quickly and easily. Fact-checking and seeking out diverse sources of information can help to counteract the effects of these biases and promote more accurate and informed decision-making. The availability heuristic is a mental shortcut that people use to make judgements and decisions based on the information that comes to mind most easily or readily. Below are some examples of the availability heuristic in relation to fake news in India.

WhatsApp forwards: In India, WhatsApp is widely used as a source of news, and many people tend to believe what they receive through WhatsApp forwards. Fake news and misinformation can easily spread through these forwards, and people may not take the time to fact-check the information they receive. This can lead to the spread of false information and can contribute to misunderstandings and even violence. For example, in 2018, several mob lynchings took place in India as a result of false rumours spread through WhatsApp. The rumours claimed that child kidnappers were on the prowl and urged people to take action against them.[1] These rumours were completely false, but they spread quickly and resulted in the deaths of several innocent people.

Social media posts: Another example of the availability heuristic in India is the spread of fake news through social media platforms like Facebook and Twitter. In recent years, India has seen a rise in fake news stories and propaganda aimed at influencing public opinion. For example, during the 2019 Indian general election, there were numerous instances of fake news being spread through social media platforms. These stories ranged from false claims about political candidates to conspiracy theories about voting machines being rigged.

In both of these examples, people tend to believe the information that is most readily available to them, rather than taking the time to fact-check or verify the information they receive. This can lead to the spread of false information and can have serious consequences for individuals and society as a whole.

Non-probative photos:[2] Non-probative photos, which are photos that do not provide direct evidence for or against a particular belief, can still have a significant impact when it comes to shaping our beliefs. This is because our brains are wired to process visual information quickly and efficiently, often relying on heuristics or mental shortcuts to make sense of what we see. One way that non-probative photos can shape our beliefs is through the phenomenon of confirmation bias. When we encounter a non-probative photo that seems to support our beliefs, we may be more likely to accept it as evidence, even if it is not actually probative. Non-probative photos can also shape belief through the availability heuristic, which refers to our tendency to judge the likelihood of an event based on how easily we can bring examples of it to mind. When we see non-probative photos that seem to depict a particular event or phenomenon, we may be more likely to believe that the event or phenomenon is widespread.

Finally, non-probative photos can shape belief through the power of visual storytelling. Photos can convey emotion and evoke empathy in a way that words alone often cannot. When we see a non-probative photo that tells a compelling story or captures a powerful emotion, we may be more likely to believe that the story or emotion is representative of a larger trend or phenomenon. In summary, non-probative photos can shape belief through confirmation bias, the availability heuristic and the power of visual storytelling. It is important to be aware of these biases and to critically evaluate any evidence, including non-probative photos, before accepting it as true.

It may look cool, but it is fake. This dangerous-looking picture of a pilot leaning out of the cockpit and taking a selfie mid-air is actually photoshopped and is quite misleading.

These photos may be used to create a sense of 'truthiness', which is a term coined by comedian Stephen Colbert to describe a feeling of truthiness that is not necessarily based on actual facts. Non-probative photos can indeed produce truthiness by creating an illusion of evidence. When people see an image that appears to support their beliefs or

Source: '30 Fake Viral Photos People Believed Were Real', Boredpanda[3]

emotions, they may assume that the image is evidence of the truth of their position. This can be particularly powerful when the image is emotionally charged or vivid, as it can override critical thinking and scepticism. However, it is important to note that the use of non-probative photos to create truth is a form of propaganda and not a valid method of argumentation. It is important to rely on actual evidence and facts when making claims or arguments, instead of relying on emotional appeals and non-probative photos.

Non-probative photos can have a significant impact on youth, both positive and negative. On the positive side, non-probative photos can be a source of inspiration and motivation. For example, seeing images of successful athletes, musicians or entrepreneurs can inspire young people to pursue their own dreams and goals. Non-probative photos can also be a way for youth to express themselves creatively, by sharing photos of their own experiences, interests and perspectives on social media. However, on the negative side, non-probative photos can contribute to the spread of misinformation, stereotypes and unrealistic standards. For example, youth may be exposed to manipulated images of people that have been heavily edited to conform to unrealistic beauty standards. This can lead to body dissatisfaction and low self-esteem. Non-probative photos can also perpetuate harmful stereotypes, such as racial or gender stereotypes that can negatively impact the way youth view themselves and others. Overall, it's important for youth to be critical consumers of non-probative photos and to understand that not everything they see on social media or the internet is necessarily true or accurate. Encouraging media literacy skills and fostering a positive body image and self-esteem can also help youth navigate the impact of non-probative photos.

Dove—Self-Esteem Project[4]

The Dove brand, which is valued at approximately $5.1 billion worldwide and commands a market share of almost 12 per cent in India, largely owes its success to its impactful advertising over the years and its positioning strategy.

From the cheesy advertisement 'Is it Love? No, it is Dove', it has come a long way to address women's self-esteem and challenge notions of 'real beauty'. The concept originated in 2002 and continues to remain a cornerstone of Dove's branding and positioning strategy.

Historically, beauty product advertisements using non-probative photographs and videos showed young, thin and white female models, setting unrealistic standards of beauty which resulted in deep discontent among women. These advertisements not only taunted women for not meeting these standards but were also uninspiring. Dove conducted focused group research involving 3000 women in ten countries. The findings revealed that only 2 per cent of the women considered themselves beautiful. This led Dove to realize that beauty brands were creating unachievable aspirations. Consequently, Dove moved away from portraying unattainable and stereotypical images of beauty and dispelled the notion that these products can turn individuals into supermodels. They conducted self-esteem workshops for women and launched a campaign for real beauty. Unilever crafted a mission statement to unify the creative expressions of the 'Real Beauty' campaign, which states, 'Dove's mission is to make more women feel beautiful every day by broadening the narrow definition of beauty and inspiring them to take great care of themselves.'

To drive traffic to their self-esteem workshops, Dove made a 112-second short film that showed how cosmetics, hairstyles and Photoshop can transform an ordinary-looking model into a billboard figure. The Dove's 'Real

Beauty' campaign launched in 2004, featured a series of ads and videos that showcased women of different ages, shapes, and ethnicities, with the tagline 'Real Beauty' prominently featured. One of the most well-known elements of the campaign was the use of real women as models, rather than professional models or actresses, and the campaign also aimed to celebrate women's natural beauty. The campaign was a huge success and garnered widespread attention and acclaim for Dove, with many people praising the brand for promoting body positivity and challenging unrealistic beauty standards. However, the campaign also faced criticism from some who felt that it was still reinforcing beauty norms by featuring conventionally attractive women and perpetuating the idea that beauty is an important measure of a woman's worth. Overall, the Dove Real Beauty campaign has been influential in promoting a more inclusive and diverse definition of beauty in the advertising industry, and it has inspired other brands to follow suit and showcase a wider range of women's bodies and appearances in their advertising.

Continuing even now, the Dove self-esteem project states on their website, 'At Dove, we believe no young person should be held back from reaching their full potential. However, low body confidence and anxieties over appearance keep young people from being their best selves, affecting their health, friendships, and even performance at school.' The Dove Self-Esteem Project offers a range of educational resources, tools and workshops that focus on building self-esteem and body confidence, particularly among young girls. These resources include online tools and activities, videos, lesson plans and guides for parents, teachers and mentors. The project has also partnered with various organizations, including the World Association of Girl Guides and Girl Scouts, to deliver workshops and programmes that promote positive body image and self-esteem. The project also conducts research and advocacy work to raise awareness of the impact of negative body image on mental health. The Dove Self-Esteem Project has been widely recognized for its positive impact on girls' and women's self-esteem, including receiving several awards and honours for its work in promoting positive body image and self-esteem.

Given the powerful effects of non-probative information, as seen in beauty advertisements or other forms of aspirational stereotypical imagery, it raises the question: How can truthiness be reduced?

'Truthiness' refers to a term coined by Stephen Colbert to describe the phenomenon where people believe something to be true because it feels right or aligns with their beliefs, rather than because of evidence or logical reasoning.[5]

There are several conditions that can make people susceptible to truthiness:

1. **Emotional reasoning:** People may be more likely to believe something that aligns with their emotions, rather than with objective facts. For example, someone might believe a conspiracy theory because it makes them feel important or special.

2. **Confirmation bias:** People tend to seek out information that confirms their existing beliefs while ignoring information that contradicts them. This can make people more likely to accept information that aligns with their beliefs, regardless of its veracity.

3. **Cognitive dissonance:** When people encounter information that contradicts their beliefs, it can create an uncomfortable feeling of cognitive dissonance. To alleviate this discomfort, people may be more likely to accept information that aligns with their existing beliefs.

4. **Lack of critical thinking skills:** People who have not developed strong critical thinking skills may be more susceptible to truthiness. They may not have the ability to evaluate evidence critically or to identify logical fallacies.

5. **Lack of knowledge:** People who are not well-informed about a particular topic may be more likely to accept information that aligns with their preconceptions, rather than seeking out accurate information.

6. **Tribalism:** People may be more likely to believe something that aligns with their social group, rather than objective facts. This can create an 'us vs them' mentality where people reject information that comes from outside their group.

Overall, people can be susceptible to truth under a variety of conditions and it's important to be aware of these factors when evaluating information. It's important to seek out accurate information and to critically evaluate claims, rather than simply accepting information that feels right.

Dunning–Kruger effect: The Dunning–Kruger effect is a cognitive bias that refers to people's tendency to overestimate their abilities in areas where they lack expertise or knowledge. In other words, people who are incompetent in a certain domain tend to believe that they are more competent than they really are. Conversely, people who are highly competent in a certain domain tend to underestimate their abilities.[6]

The Dunning–Kruger effect can be relevant to the spread of fake news, which is information that is intentionally misleading or false. People who lack knowledge or expertise in a certain area may be more susceptible to believing fake news because they may not have the skills to evaluate the accuracy of the information. Additionally, people who overestimate their knowledge or abilities may be more likely to share or promote fake news because they believe they are knowledgeable enough to recognize any possible misinformation.

Furthermore, people who overestimate their abilities may be more susceptible to becoming victims of fake news themselves. They may believe that they have enough knowledge or expertise to recognize and reject fake news when they see it, but in reality, their lack of understanding of the subject matter may make them vulnerable to manipulation. Overall, the Dunning–Kruger effect can play a role in the spread of fake news by making people more vulnerable to misinformation and making it harder for them to recognize accurate information. It is important to be aware of this bias and to continually evaluate one's own knowledge and expertise in order to avoid falling victim to fake news.

One hilarious example of people not reading the complete story and commenting on the post was when National Public Radio of USA posted a satirical piece, titled 'Why doesn't America read anymore?'. Upon clicking on the link, readers would be told it was just an April Fools' Day joke. The irony was lost on many people who commented angrily on the post without bothering to read what was written.

This is not an isolated incident, as people mostly tend to engage with a post based on its headline rather than its content. This is alarming, as a study found that 2.8 million online news articles were shared and commented on without opening the link to read the story.[7] So, what makes a message feel true? In our regular conversational conduct, we believe that a messenger is a cooperative communicator in the group and that his views and opinions are going to add value to the group's conversational process. This is why we generally retweet a post without reading it, unless we find an element of doubt in the message itself which makes us open and read the link in detail to filter fake information from truth.

In India, some political leaders are known for making outrageous statements and demonstrating an obvious lack of knowledge on certain key issues. This could be attributed to the Dunning–Kruger effect, as they may believe they have a greater understanding of the topic than they actually do and end up creating and spreading fake information. In recent years, social media has given rise to a new breed of influencers who often have no formal training or education in the fields they are promoting. They may overestimate their abilities and knowledge and present themselves as experts in their field and may promote views that lack factual basis and may lead their followers to believe in whatever false information their favourite influencer might be promoting. In India, some religious leaders may overestimate their knowledge and understanding of scripture, leading them to make inaccurate or incorrect interpretations. This is yet another example of the Dunning–Kruger effect. Such a mindset may lead to a lot of false information floating in society and may even lead to clashes between two different religious factions.

Illusory truth effect:[8] The illusory truth effect is a cognitive bias that causes people to perceive information as more truthful after repeated exposure to it, regardless of its actual validity. This bias is related to the fact that familiarity often breeds comfort and trust. People are more likely to accept information as true when they have heard it before, regardless of whether it is actually accurate or not. The illusory truth effect is particularly relevant in the context of fake news because false information can be spread widely and repeatedly through social media and other channels, leading many people to believe it is true. As a result, fake news can have a significant impact on public opinion and decision-making. The illusory truth effect can also be exacerbated by confirmation bias, which is the tendency to search for, interpret and remember information in a way that confirms one's pre-existing beliefs and biases. When people encounter information that confirms what they already believe, they are more likely to accept it as true and less likely to question its accuracy. Here are some examples of illusory truth and fake news:

1. **Illusory truth:** 'The earth is flat.' Despite centuries of knowledge and overwhelming scientific evidence of the earth being spherical, a small but vocal group of people has continued to assert that the earth is flat. This has led some people to believe that there could be a legitimate debate about the shape of the earth.

2. **Fake news:** 'COVID-19 vaccines cause infertility.' This claim has been widely circulated on social media and other online platforms, despite there being no evidence to support it. In fact, numerous studies have shown that COVID-19 vaccines are safe and effective.

3. **Illusory truth:** 'More guns make us safer.' This claim is often repeated by advocates of gun ownership, despite evidence to the contrary. In reality, countries with strict gun laws tend to have significantly lower rates of gun violence.

4. **Fake news:** 'Hillary Clinton ran a child sex ring out of the basement of a pizzeria.' This conspiracy theory

was widely circulated during the 2016 US presidential election, despite having no basis in reality. It led to a man firing a gun in the restaurant in question, endangering the lives of innocent people.

5. **Illusory truth:** 'You only use 10 per cent of your brain.' This claim has been made in several movies and TV shows over the years, leading many people to believe it to be true. However, it is a complete myth. In reality, we use all parts of our brain, just not all at the same time.

False information and rumours spread through social media platforms like WhatsApp can create an illusory truth effect. For example, during the COVID-19 pandemic, there were several misleading messages being forwarded on WhatsApp, which claimed that certain medicines or remedies could cure the disease. Many people believed these messages, even though there was no scientific evidence to support them.

Political parties are known to use propaganda to influence public opinion. This can create an illusory truth effect, where people believe false or misleading information to be true because they have heard it repeatedly. For example, during the 2019 Indian general elections, some political parties used false claims about their opponents to discredit them and gain votes. Indian history is not far away from illusory truths as historical myths and legends can also create an illusory truth effect. For example, the myth that the Taj Mahal was originally a Hindu temple called Tejo Mahalaya has been widely circulated in India.[9] Despite there being no historical evidence to support this claim, many people believe it to be true because they have heard it so often.

Are you superstitious? We all have some belief in superstition or maybe we don't! Superstitions are beliefs or practices that are not based on scientific evidence. They can create an illusory truth effect, where people believe in them simply because they have heard them repeated so often. For example, some people believe that breaking a mirror brings seven years of bad luck or that black cats are unlucky. These beliefs lack evidence, yet many people believe them to be true.

These are just a few examples of how illusory truth and fake news can influence our beliefs and perceptions. It is important to be critical of the information we encounter and to seek out reliable sources to verify claims. In conclusion, the illusory truth effect is a cognitive bias that can make people more likely to believe fake news if they are exposed to it repeatedly. It is important for individuals to be aware of this bias and to actively seek out diverse sources of information to avoid being misled by false or misleading information.

Social influence is another important factor in the spread of fake news. People tend to be influenced by the opinions and behaviours of others in their social networks. When fake news is shared by people they trust or admire, people may be more likely to believe and share it themselves. Emotional responses also play a role in the psychology of fake news. Fake news stories often rely on sensational or emotionally charged content to grab people's attention and evoke strong emotional responses, such as fear or anger. These emotions can make people more likely to believe and share false information. Social influence is indeed a crucial factor in the spread of fake news. Social influence refers to the way in which people's thoughts, feelings and behaviours are influenced by the people around them. In the context of fake news, social influence can take many forms, including:

Social endorsement: When people see others sharing or endorsing a piece of information, particularly friends and family on the social media network, they are more likely to believe it. This is known as social proof, and it can be a powerful driver of belief. In 2018, a spate of lynchings occurred across India, where people were beaten to death by mobs who believed they were child kidnappers. These incidents were sparked by fake messages being spread on WhatsApp, which claimed that gangs were roaming around the country abducting children.[10]

In January 2020, a group of masked men attacked students and faculty at Jawaharlal Nehru University (JNU) in New Delhi.[11] Soon after the attack, social media was flooded with fake news and misinformation, with some users claiming that the attack was staged and others accusing the victims of being members of a left-wing extremist group.[12]

In March 2020, the Tablighi Jamaat, a Muslim missionary movement, was blamed for spreading COVID-19 in India. False reports were circulated on social media, claiming that the organization was deliberately spreading the virus.[13] These rumours led to a wave of hatred and violence against Muslims in India.

In 2021, farmers in India began protesting against three new agricultural laws passed by the government. Social media was flooded with misinformation and fake news about the protests, with some users claiming that the protests were being funded by foreign actors and others accusing the protesters of being terrorists.

These are just a few examples of how social endorsement can be used to spread fake news and misinformation in India. It is important to be vigilant and fact-check information before sharing it on social media.

Group polarization: When people engage in discussions with like-minded peers, their opinions often become more extreme over time. This can lead to the spread of fake news and misinformation within the group.

Authority bias: People are often more likely to believe information when it comes from a perceived authority figure, such as a politician, expert or celebrity.

Emotional contagion: When people see others reacting emotionally to a piece of information, they are more likely to experience the same emotions themselves. This can lead to the spread of fake news that triggers strong emotional responses, such as outrage or fear.

All of these social influences can contribute to the spread of fake news and misinformation, making it more difficult to combat. It's important to be aware of these influences and to critically evaluate information before sharing it with others.

Overall, the psychology of fake news is complex and multifaceted, and it requires a deep understanding of human cognition, social dynamics and emotional responses. Understanding these factors can help us develop strategies to counter the spread of fake news and promote more informed, evidence-based decision-making.

Negative Bias in the Judgement of Truth

Consider the following two statements: '80 per cent of marriages last ten years or more' and '20 per cent of marriages end in divorce before their tenth year'. Although both statements convey the same information, individuals' assessment of the statements may differ based on whether they register the positive statement or negative statement as per their frame of reference. According to Benjamin Hilbig's research (2009) titled, 'Sad, thus true: Negative bias in judgment of truth', people tend to believe the second statement to be truer—'20 per cent of marriages end in a divorce before their tenth year'.[14]

Let's understand it better: negativity bias is a cognitive phenomenon where negative information tends to have a stronger impact on judgements and decisions as compared to positive information. This bias has been widely observed in various domains, including the evaluation of information for its truthiness. Studies have shown that emotional arousal can influence how people evaluate the truthiness of information, with negative emotions leading to a greater sensitivity to deception. Another perspective is to examine the cognitive mechanisms underlying the negativity bias. For example, recent research has suggested that the negativity bias may be driven by a general tendency to pay more attention to information that is inconsistent with one's expectations or prior beliefs. This means that people may be more likely to view negative information as true because it goes against their expectations or beliefs.

Overall, these new perspectives on the negativity bias in judgements of truth highlight the complexity of this phenomenon and suggest that it is influenced by a variety of factors, including emotions, cognitive processes, and social and cultural norms. By understanding these factors, researchers can develop more effective strategies for promoting accurate judgements of truth in various contexts.

Are False Beliefs Byproducts of Our Adaptive Knowledge Base?

With the widespread prevalence of fake news in our lives, it is almost impossible to eliminate all of the false information that we encounter every day, as it is amplified through social media. Many times, fake news is crafted to exploit people's emotions and religious sentiments through slogans such as 'Hindu *khatre mein hai*' (Hindus are in danger). Fake news of this kind can instil fear among people and portray minority Muslim populations as a threat.

This 'Hot Cognition' is a result of our cognitive processes continuously updating our knowledge and beliefs about Indian society. Believing in fake news thus becomes a natural part of our cognitive process and is no longer a deliberate strategy adopted by the individual. Our knowledge and beliefs are shaped over time from discrete knowledge ranging from who is the hero of a movie to scripts developed from past experiences such as driving a car.

False beliefs formulated by fake news need to be corrected through factual information. Consider the so-called 'originism' debate surrounding UK Prime Minister Rishi Sunak. Though Rishi Sunak's grandparents came from British India, their birthplace is Gujranwala, which is now in Pakistan. Both India and Pakistan are now claiming his origin as their own, sparking a war of claims on Twitter where Pakistanis are claiming that a man from their country has been voted to the highest office in the United Kingdom. One person even went ahead to advise Rishi Sunak to now return the Kohinoor Diamond which was stolen from Lahore. So those from India believe that Mr Sunak is of Indian origin while those from Pakistan believe that he is of Pakistan origin. All this is because we are biased by our reference points of information.

Those who were not supporting US President Barack Obama would tend to believe stories like 'Clint Eastwood Refuses to Accept presidential Medal of Freedom from Obama, Says He Is Not My President'.

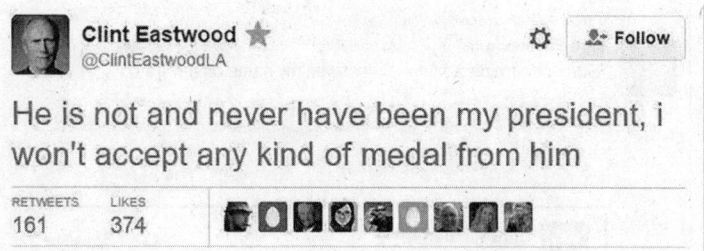

Source: 'Did Clint Eastwood Refuse the presidential Medal of Freedom?'[15]

Fact-checking website Snopes rated the story as 'false' and that the @ClintEastwoodLA account is not associated with the Hollywood icon. Later on, the actor's official Twitter handle clarified that the tweet was put out by a fake profile. According to Obama, 'The presidential Medal of Freedom is not just our nation's highest civilian honour—it's a tribute to the idea that all of us, no matter where we come from, have the opportunity to change this country for the better. From scientists, philanthropists, and public servants to activists, athletes, and artists, these 21 individuals have helped push America forward, inspiring millions of people around the world along the way.' In 2010, Clint Eastwood was conferred with the 'National Medals for Arts' award. Though he did not attend the ceremony, he never rejected the honour bestowed on him.

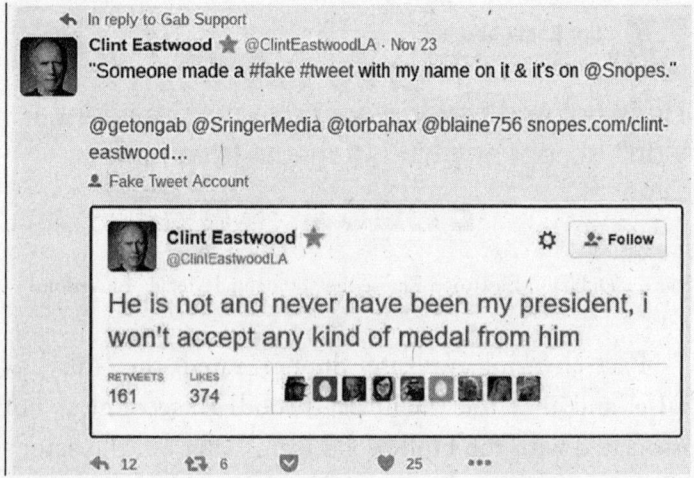

Source: 'Did Clint Eastwood Refuse the presidential Medal of Freedom?'[16]

This bias to believe in fake news stems from the 'cognitive laziness' of the participant. 'Cognitive laziness' is a term used to describe a tendency to avoid mental effort or to rely on mental shortcuts instead of engaging in more thoughtful and deliberate cognitive processes. It can manifest in various ways, such as procrastination, avoidance of challenging tasks or a preference for simple and easy solutions over more complex or nuanced ones. People may become cognitively lazy for a variety of reasons, including lack of motivation, fear of failure or a desire to conserve mental energy. However, this tendency can have negative consequences, such as reduced productivity, lower quality of work and missed opportunities for personal growth and development. Individuals who apply logic and reasoning in processing information are more likely to reject fake news as compared to their 'cognitively lazy' counterparts. For example, the one who answered incorrectly the question, 'How much mud is there in a hole that is 3 ft deep x 3 ft wide x 3 ft long?' is more likely to believe in fake news headlines despite the correct answer being that there is no mud in a hole.

Also, people tend to take shortcuts in processing information or news. The more easy-to-process news tends to be true as compared to the complex news stories which are difficult to process and understand. For people to understand it better, fake news items are generally repeated frequently. *Did Indian Prime Minister Narendra Modi stop the Russia–Ukraine war for 72 hours to evacuate 35,000 Indians?* Many believed this to be true as it was repeatedly claimed by several prominent ruling party BJP leaders on their social media handles and in media interviews.[17]

Alt-News did a fact check and found it to be a false claim as the external affairs spokesperson Arindam Bagchi had denied in an internal briefing that the Russia–Ukraine war was stopped at the Prime Minister's behest. Addressing a press conference, Bagchi said, 'We got specific inputs that look . . . this is a route that's available . . . these are the places that Indian citizens should go by this time. We conveyed that to our citizens. And I am happy that many could make it . . . there were sporadic incidents of violence, but this is a war zone and I can't comment on the details. We haven't met them yet . . . But I am happy that a significant number of people could come out . . . Extrapolating that to say that somebody is holding up bombing or this is something we are coordinating, [that] I think that's absolutely inaccurate.'[18]

The repetition of information from a credible source like the BJP's top brass can lead individuals to believe it is true. So how can we as citizens be more 'cognitively active'? To overcome cognitive laziness and be more aware and active in consuming news and information, one can cultivate habits of mindfulness, goal-setting and deliberate practice. Developing a growth mindset can also be helpful, as it encourages individuals to embrace challenges and view failure as an opportunity for learning and growth.

It is interesting to know that fake news revolves around real people and real issues. Individuals incorporate knowledge from fake news into their own perceptions based on their existing biases and add it to their existing beliefs. The individual uses fake news to fill in their existing knowledge gaps based on their existing beliefs as they may do with any other piece of information. Because of 'cognitive laziness', these fake news interpretations can persist until a credible source clears the doubts or the individual becomes aware and seeks the truth.

Knowledge is more 'known' than 'remembered', often applied without revisiting events that formed that knowledge. For example, people know that Jawaharlal Nehru was the first Prime Minister of India. They will not go back to the events that formed this knowledge for them, whereas a more research-oriented, fact-checking mind will gather all the facts and remember the sequence of events that formed this knowledge. Sometimes, despite correctly evaluating the source of information, we are quick to apply our existing knowledge rather than consulting our memory. For example, we are used to spelling certain words wrong despite having had to correct ourselves in the past.

As we know, information trickles down from many sources and the fact that some may have come from less credited sources does not matter, particularly in the digital era. One instance of this can be seen with Wikipedia, which many individuals rely on for information without knowing or caring that it is a crowdsourced website, where pages can be created by any individual or organization.

Reliance on gadgets like mobile phones and computers has reduced the use of memory and cognitive skills. Training the brain and retrieving information from memory can enhance cognitive abilities.

People are capable of learning huge amounts of information and retaining them in their memory. The pervasiveness of fake news on social media makes it almost impossible to stop its amplification. Though social media platforms like Facebook and Google are tweaking their algorithms to identify and stop the dissemination of fake news, their efforts are not foolproof and have often backfired. The other way to control the spread of fake news is to fact-check it through websites like www.snopes.com or www.altnews.com. Though they are effective, their usage and scope remain a matter of question. Governments can also come up with legislative changes to stop the creation and dissemination of fake news. In India, implementation of legislation is challenging as it is difficult to identify real from fake and also due to the presence of legal loopholes. The gravity of fake news can be gauged from the fact that Chief Justice of India D.Y. Chandrachud himself had once referred to fake news as a tool for creating communal tensions and one that can endanger democratic values in society.[19]

V

How Memes Stir Up Fake News

'Memes can be dangerous when they spread misinformation, hate or harmful stereotypes. We need to be careful about what we share and how it affects others.'

—Tim Berners-Lee,
inventor of the World Wide Web

There was a time in India when political parties would drop election leaflets and pamphlets using helicopters in densely populated areas. This was done by all parties, with the ruling party particularly using this strategy to highlight their achievements and their stated goals. They believed that the airdrop of this material would generate curiosity and prompt people to read it as compared to any other vehicle used for marketing or communication.[1] Memes on social media have become the modern-day equivalent of pamphlets. Once air dropped, these memes are now strategically planted in social media feeds as part of psychological operations (PSYOP) tactics, aiming to influence people's perceptions of current situations, issues and individuals.

Internet memes are a unique form of digital communication that have the power to spread rapidly and shape public discourse. A meme is a humorous or provocative image, video or text that is often shared across social media platforms and messaging apps. Memes can take on a life of their own, as people adapt and remix them to reflect new contexts or trends.[2]

One reason why memes are so powerful is that they tap into our collective experiences and emotions. They often reference pop culture, current events or shared cultural references, allowing people to quickly connect and relate to each other. They can also be used to express complex ideas or critiques in a simple and accessible way, making them a popular tool for political and social commentary. Their viral nature is another key factor contributing to their influence. Designed to be shared and reshared easily, with small modifications or adaptations, memes are highly adaptable and flexible, often spreading quickly across online communities and reaching far beyond their original creators. They can also be used as a powerful tool for social change—to raise awareness about important issues, challenge dominant narratives or call attention to social injustices. By harnessing the power of humour and visual imagery, memes can bring attention to complex social issues in a way that is engaging and accessible to a wide audience.

Memes can potentially stir up fake news by distorting or misrepresenting information in a way that is easily shareable and attention grabbing. They are often designed to be humorous, provocative or emotional, and they can quickly spread through social media platforms and messaging apps. Since memes are typically created by individuals or groups without any fact-checking or editorial oversight, they can easily incorporate false or misleading information. Additionally, they often rely on simplifications, exaggerations and stereotypes to make a point, which can further contribute to the spread of inaccurate information. When memes are shared widely and rapidly, they can influence people's opinions and beliefs, even if they are based on misinformation. This can create a ripple effect, where false information spreads rapidly and becomes accepted as truth, leading to potential negative consequences for individuals, organizations or society as a whole.

So, when Rahul Gandhi of the Congress party in India took a morning run with his supporters in Telangana during the Bharat Jodo Yatra, the video went viral and became the target of many memes circulated on social media.

Though memes are created to create humour and laughs, here it was intended to dilute the impact and purpose of the Bharat Jodo Yatra.

So why is it done? Social learning theory is indeed one psychological theory that can be used to explain the spread and impact of memes. According to social learning theory, people learn new behaviours by observing and imitating

← **Tweet**

The Jaipur Dialogues ✓
@JaipurDialogues   ...

Rahul Gandhi running off his political responsibilities like...

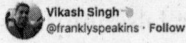

Vikash Singh 🐦
@franklyspeakins · **Follow**

Forest Gump who does not know why he is running 😀😀😀
@RahulGandhi @INCIndia
#LaalSinghChaddha #AmirKhan

53rd Day | 1350+ KM | Energy Level 🔥

6:47 AM · Oct 31, 2022   ⓘ

Source: News18[3]

others. This can include the adoption of new beliefs, values and attitudes, as well as the replication of specific actions or behaviours.

When it comes to memes, social learning theory suggests that people are more likely to adopt and share memes that are consistent with their existing beliefs and values, as well as those that they perceive to be popular or socially desirable. Memes that are easy to understand and remember, and those that generate a strong emotional response, are also more likely to be spread. In addition to social learning theory, other psychological theories that have been used to explain the spread and impact of memes include cognitive dissonance theory, which suggests that people are motivated to reduce the discomfort of holding contradictory beliefs, and social identity theory, which suggests that people are more likely to adopt and share memes that are consistent with their group identities.

Internet memes have become an increasingly popular form of communication in the digital age. While memes are often used for entertainment purposes, they can also be used as tools of propaganda.

Propaganda is a technique used to influence people's beliefs, attitudes or behaviours. It is often associated with government or political campaigns, but it can also be used by individuals, organizations and corporations. Propaganda can take many forms, including advertising, news media and social media.

Internet memes can be used as a form of propaganda because they are easily shared and have the potential to reach a large audience. Memes can be created to promote a particular agenda, spread false information or attack a political opponent. They can also be used to reinforce stereotypes or promote divisive ideas.

For example, during the 2016 US presidential election, the campaign teams of both Donald Trump and Hillary Clinton used memes to reach younger voters. While the Trump campaign used memes to attack his opponents and promote his message, the Clinton campaign used memes to humanize the candidate and connect with younger voters.[4]

Memes can also be used to spread false information or conspiracy theories. For example, during the COVID-19 pandemic, memes were shared that promoted the idea that the virus was a hoax or that wearing masks was unnecessary.[5] These memes can be dangerous because they can lead to people disregarding public health guidelines and putting themselves and others at risk.

Internet memes have the potential to be powerful tools of propaganda. While memes can be used for entertainment purposes, it is important to be aware of their potential impact on our beliefs and attitudes. It is important to critically evaluate memes before sharing them and to be mindful of their potential to spread false information or promote divisive ideas.

Here are some of the memes which are a hilarious representation of the political debate in India:

1. **'Aloo vs. Onion':** This meme emerged after the prices of onions skyrocketed in India, and people began

comparing the high prices of onions to the low prices of potatoes. The meme became popular and was used to criticize the government's inability to control the rising prices of essential commodities.[6]

2. **'Rahul Gandhi Hugging Modi':** This meme became popular after opposition leader Rahul Gandhi walked across the benches and hugged Prime Minister Narendra Modi in the middle of a debate in Parliament. The hug was seen as a sign of political unity and was widely discussed on social media.[7]

3. **'Chowkidar Chor Hai':** This meme emerged during the 2019 Indian general elections after Rahul Gandhi accused Prime Minister Narendra Modi of being corrupt. The meme soon became popular among opposition parties and was used extensively on social media platforms.[8]

4. **'Pappu vs. Feku':** This meme became popular during the 2014 Indian general elections, referring to Rahul Gandhi as 'pappu' (a derogatory term used to describe someone who is daft) and Narendra Modi as 'feku' (a term used to describe someone who boasts excessively). The meme was widely shared on social media and became a symbol of the intense rivalry between the two leaders.[9]

It's worth noting that political memes can be controversial and often reflect the biases and opinions of the creators. It's important to be critical of the information presented in memes and to fact-check any claims before sharing them on social media. Memes are often used as a tool to spread misinformation and disinformation because they are easy to create, share and consume on social media platforms. Here are some ways memes are used to spread false information:

Manipulation of images: Memes often use manipulated images to create a false narrative or to misrepresent facts. These images can be taken out of context, edited to change their meaning or manipulated to appear authentic. Memes use manipulated images as a way to convey a message or express humour. The images used in memes are usually taken from popular culture, such as movies, TV shows and video games, and then altered or combined with text to create a new meaning or context. Manipulated images in memes can range from simple edits, such as adding text to a photo or changing the colour of an object, to more complex edits, such as combining multiple images or photoshopping elements together to create a new scene. The use of manipulated images in memes has become a popular form of internet culture and has been used to comment on a wide range of topics, from politics and social issues to popular trends and memes themselves.

Here are some examples of memes that manipulate images for comedic or persuasive effect:[10]

1. **'Distracted Boyfriend':** This popular meme features a stock photo of a man turning his head to check out another woman while his girlfriend looks on in disapproval. The image is often repurposed with

different captions to depict various situations where someone is distracted by something more interesting than what they're supposed to be focusing on.

2. **'Hotline Bling':** The image features rapper Drake in a video still from his song 'Hotline Bling', where he is shown dancing awkwardly. The image is often used to portray moments of indecision, awkwardness or discomfort.

3. **'SpongeBob SquarePants':** This meme uses images from the animated TV series of the same name to portray a variety of humorous situations. For example, an image of SpongeBob with his eyes wide open and a crazed expression is often used to depict shock or excitement.

4. **'The Most Interesting Man in the World':** This meme features an image of a suave-looking older man, accompanied by the phrase 'I don't always [do something], but when I do, I end up [doing something else].' The meme is used to make fun of people who think they're sophisticated or worldly-wise.

5. **'Change My Mind':** This meme features an image of conservative political commentator Steven Crowder sitting at a table with a sign that says 'Male privilege is a myth, change my mind.' The image is often repurposed with different signs and captions to promote different viewpoints or ideas.

While memes can be a powerful tool for communication and social commentary, they can also be used to manipulate public opinion and perpetuate harmful stereotypes. It is essential to exercise caution and critical thinking while consuming and sharing memes.

Satirical or ironic memes: Satirical or ironic memes are a form of online humour that use satire or irony to comment on a particular topic or issue. They often employ humorous images, captions and text to make a statement or convey a message in a way that is intended to be amusing, but also thought-provoking. These types of memes are often used to criticize or mock political figures, social issues, cultural trends or even other memes themselves. They can be a powerful tool for social commentary and can help to raise awareness of important issues while also providing entertainment. Satirical or ironic memes can be used to convey false information in a humorous way. This can be dangerous as some people may not realize that the meme is not meant to be taken seriously.

However, satirical or ironic memes can be controversial and offensive to some people, particularly if they touch on sensitive topics or target specific groups. As with any form of humour, it's important to consider the potential impact of these memes on others and to use them responsibly. Some examples of satirical or ironic memes:

1. 'I'm not saying I'm Batman. I'm just saying no one has ever seen me and Batman in the same room together.' This meme plays on the idea that people who claim to

be Batman are likely not actually Batman, but rather fans who wish they were.

2. 'When you accidentally type 'you're' instead of 'your', but your auto-correct doesn't correct you.' This meme is ironic because the person is making fun of someone else's grammar mistake while making one themselves.

3. 'When you finally finish a book, but the plot twist was so unexpected that you need a minute to process it.' This meme is satirical because it pokes fun at the idea that readers are often portrayed as being shocked by plot twists, when in reality they may have seen them coming.

4. 'When you hear someone say they don't like pizza.' This meme is ironic because it shows a dramatic reaction to someone expressing an opinion that is not really that controversial.

5. 'When you get all dressed up to go out, but then you realize you're an introvert and would rather stay home.' This meme is satirical because it plays on the stereotype that introverts prefer to stay home rather than go out and socialize.

Clickbait: Memes can be used as clickbait to lure people to websites or social media pages that promote false information. These memes may contain sensational or shocking content to attract attention and encourage people to click on the link. Clickbait memes are memes that are designed to be catchy and attention-grabbing in order to entice people to click on them. These memes often use provocative or sensational headlines, images or captions to lure viewers into clicking through to a website or social media post. Clickbait memes can be used for a variety of purposes, including driving traffic to a website, generating ad revenue or promoting a particular product or service. However, they are often criticized for being misleading or deceptive, as they may promise one thing but deliver something else entirely. Examples of clickbait memes might include a meme with an attention-grabbing headline like 'You won't believe what this cat did!' or a meme with an image of a celebrity accompanied by a provocative caption like 'You won't believe who this star is dating now!' There are many other examples too:

1. This man lost 50 pounds in one month using this one weird trick!
2. The top 10 most shocking celebrity transformations!
3. You'll never guess what happened next in this viral video!
4. This woman's incredible makeup transformation will leave you speechless!
5. The ultimate life hack that will change your mornings forever!
6. This simple trick will save you hundreds of dollars on your grocery bill!
7. You won't believe what this bridezilla did on her wedding day!
8. The most hilarious memes that will make you laugh out loud!

9. This one simple ingredient will transform your cooking game forever!

Conspiracy theories: Memes are often used to promote conspiracy theories that are not based on facts. These memes can be shared widely on social media platforms and can reach a large audience quickly. Memes are a popular way to share ideas, and they can spread quickly and widely through social media platforms. Unfortunately, some people use memes to spread false or misleading information, including conspiracy theories. Conspiracy theories are often based on a lack of evidence or a misunderstanding of events, and they can be appealing to people who feel powerless or disenfranchised. Memes that promote conspiracy theories often use eye-catching images and slogans to grab people's attention, but they may not be based on fact. It's important to be critical of the information we see online, including memes. When we encounter a meme that promotes a conspiracy theory, we should take the time to fact-check the claims and seek out credible sources. By doing so, we can avoid being misled by false information and make informed decisions about what we believe.

While memes are typically used to convey humour or commentary on popular culture, they can also be used to spread conspiracy theories.

Here are some examples of memes that promote conspiracy theories:

1. **Jet fuel can't melt steel beams:** This meme suggests that the collapse of the Twin Towers on 9/11 was not caused by the impact of the planes, but rather a controlled demolition. It implies that the US government was involved in the attack.[11]

2. **Wake up, sheeple!** This meme suggests that the majority of people are blindly following the government or media without questioning the truth behind events and that those who do question are the only ones who are truly awake and aware of the real situation.[12]

3. **Flat earth:** This meme suggests that the Earth is not actually spherical, as scientific evidence suggests, but rather a flat disc. It implies that this information is being covered up by the government and mainstream media.[13]

4. **QAnon:** This meme promotes the conspiracy theory that a group of high-level government officials and celebrities are involved in a secret paedophilia ring and that former President Donald Trump was working to expose and bring them to justice.[14]

5. **The great reset:** This meme suggests that there is a secret plan by world leaders to use the COVID-19 pandemic as an excuse to create a one-world government and destroy individual freedoms.[15]

It's important to note that while memes can be entertaining, they can also be dangerous if they spread misinformation and promote conspiracy theories that have no basis in fact.

Partisan politics: Memes can be used to spread false information about political candidates or parties. These memes often rely on exaggeration, manipulation of images and misleading information to promote a particular agenda. It is important to be critical of the information presented in memes and to fact-check information before sharing it on social media. Memes have become a popular way for people to express their political views and opinions. Unfortunately, memes can also be used to spread misinformation and further partisan divides.

Here are a few examples of memes that have been used for American partisan politics:

1. **'Liberal Logic' memes:** These typically portray liberals as illogical or hypocritical. They often use false or exaggerated statements to criticize liberal policies and beliefs.[16]

2. **Conservative Compassion:** These memes typically portray conservatives as compassionate and caring. They often use emotional appeals to support conservative policies and beliefs.[17]

3. **Trump Train:** These memes were popular during the 2016 presidential election and portrayed Donald Trump and his supporters as a powerful force that could not be stopped.[18]

4. **Bernie Bros:** These memes were popular during the 2016 and 2020 presidential primaries and portrayed Bernie Sanders and his supporters as aggressive and sexist.[19]

5. **'NPC' memes:** These memes are a recent phenomenon and are often used to criticize liberals and progressives. They portray liberals as unthinking automatons who blindly follow the mainstream media and political elites.[20]

It's important to remember that memes can be humorous and entertaining, but they should not be taken as serious political analysis. It's always a good idea to fact-check information before sharing it online and to avoid spreading memes that promote division and hatred. Here are some partisan-politics memes from around the world:

1. **United States:** Political memes have become a staple of American political culture, particularly during election seasons. Supporters of different political parties often use memes to mock or criticize their opponents, to share political messages or to promote their preferred candidates.

2. **Russia:** In Russia, political memes are often used to criticize the government and President Vladimir Putin. Anti-Putin memes have become particularly popular in recent years, with many people using social media to express their dissatisfaction with the country's political leadership.

3. **Brazil:** Brazilian politics have become increasingly polarized in recent years, and political memes have become a popular way for supporters of different parties to engage in online battles. In particular, supporters of right-wing President Jair Bolsonaro have used

memes to criticize their opponents and to defend the president's policies.

4. **India:** Memes have become an important tool for Indian political parties to reach young voters. Both the ruling BJP and the opposition Congress party have created their own memes to engage with supporters and attack their opponents.

5. **Philippines:** President Rodrigo Duterte has a strong online presence, and his supporters often use memes to promote his policies and attack his critics. Duterte himself has also been known to share memes on social media, which has helped to fuel his popularity among younger voters.

In recent years, social media platforms have become a popular battleground for Indian partisan politics, and memes have become an effective tool for political communication and propaganda. Memes are often used to spread political messages, mock opponents and galvanize support among followers. Indian political parties and their supporters have been using memes to influence public opinion and win elections. For example, during the 2019 Indian general elections, several political parties used memes to appeal to young voters and create a buzz on social media. The use of memes in Indian partisan politics has also sparked controversy, with some arguing that memes can be used to spread fake news and misinformation. Additionally, some memes have been criticized for being offensive and promoting hate speech. Overall, memes have become an integral part of Indian partisan politics, and their impact on public opinion is likely to continue to grow as social media becomes increasingly important in political communication.

Political memes are a popular form of digital communication used to convey political messages and opinions. In India, memes are widely used by political parties and their supporters to criticize, satirize or support politicians and their policies.

For example, during the 2019 Indian general elections, memes were used extensively by political parties and their supporters to mock their opponents and highlight their own strengths.[21] Some popular memes during the election season included the 'Chowkidar' meme, which was used by the Bharatiya Janata Party (BJP) to promote their anti-corruption message, and the 'Feku' meme, which was used by the opposition Congress party to criticize the BJP's prime ministerial candidate, Narendra Modi.[22] However, it's important to note that political memes can often be divisive and inflammatory, and can contribute to a polarized political climate. It's important for individuals to critically evaluate the messages conveyed in political memes and to engage in constructive political discourse that respects different perspectives and viewpoints.

How Memes Got Weaponized

Memes are often thought of as harmless and humorous images or videos that are shared on the internet. However, they have been weaponized in various ways, primarily through the spread of disinformation and propaganda. One of the ways in which memes have been weaponized is through the use of social media platforms, which allow for the rapid dissemination of information and the creation of echo chambers. Memes can be used to spread false or misleading information, and they can be used to manipulate people's opinions and beliefs. Another way in which memes have been weaponized is through their use in political campaigns. Political parties and groups can use memes to attack their opponents or to rally support for their own cause. Memes can be used to spread negative stereotypes and to create division among different groups of people. Finally, memes have been used to spread hate speech and extremist ideologies. White supremacist groups, for example, have used memes to promote their beliefs and to recruit new members. Memes can be used to normalize hateful or violent behaviour and to desensitize people to the harm that it can cause.

For example, memes have played a significant role in spreading awareness about the Black Lives Matter movement.[23] They provide a platform for individuals to express their views on the subject in a humorous, relatable and engaging way. Memes related to the Black Lives Matter movement often depict serious issues such as police brutality, racial profiling and discrimination in a humorous and satirical way. This approach can help raise awareness among those who might not otherwise have engaged with the topic. Furthermore, the use of memes has been effective in providing a sense of community and solidarity among black individuals and their allies. It helps to bring people together by highlighting shared experiences and emotions, and this has been especially important during times of crisis and uncertainty.

Unfortunately, memes have also been used to spread fake news and misinformation about the movement. Some individuals and groups have created and shared memes that contain false information, inflammatory content or racially charged language to push their own agendas or to sow discord. For instance, some memes have misrepresented incidents of violence or police brutality against black individuals, while others have spread conspiracy theories about the origins or goals of the movement. One example of a fake meme related to the movement is the widely circulated image of George Soros, a wealthy philanthropist and political donor, as a purported sponsor of the movement. This meme falsely claimed that Soros was funding violent protests and riots associated with the movement, and it was used to discredit and delegitimize the movement. In reality, Soros has no direct involvement with the Black Lives Matter movement, which is a grassroots effort that relies on the support of individual donors and community organizations.[24] This meme was part of a larger trend of misinformation and conspiracy theories about the Black Lives Matter movement, which have been used to undermine its goals and discredit its supporters.

Similarly, during the **#MeToo** movement, memes were used by some individuals and groups to discredit or undermine the experiences of survivors of sexual harassment and assault. Some memes were designed to mock or ridicule victims, while others were created to promote conspiracy theories or misinformation about the movement itself. For example, some memes claimed that the movement was a hoax orchestrated by feminists or the media, while others suggested that false accusations of sexual harassment and assault were rampant and widespread. These claims were not only false but also harmful, as they undermined the credibility of survivors and perpetuated harmful stereotypes about women and victims of sexual violence.[25]

One example of this is the recent Johnny Depp and Amber Heard defamation lawsuit. When Amber Heard was ridiculed, humiliated and denigrated online, a precedent for online misogyny was set in the form of jokes and memes. Heard was accused of being a 'public figure representing domestic abuse' and was then sued for three counts of defamation by her ex-husband, Johnny Depp. Users of TikTok turned Heard's accounts of intimate domestic abuse into a fad for young viewers, fetishizing and acting out her story. Through their social media channels, other businesses commented on Heard's statement, including Milani and Duolingo. 'Pro-Johnny' YouTube accounts streamed the trial concurrently as though it were a live spectator sport. The events surrounding Heard and Depp's personal relationship were used as entertainment on social media, clearly painting Heard as the bad guy. However, their situation shows how #MeToo's efforts to end sexual violence have been horribly undermined by the pervasive misogynistic online cultures that still exist. Brutal depictions of sexual assault have now developed into a fun source of humour online.[26]

This example shows how memes can be used to spread false information and distort the facts, even in the context of a social movement as important and sensitive as #MeToo. It's important to fact-check information before sharing it, especially when it comes to sensitive and contentious topics like sexual assault and harassment.

All Is Not Bad with Memes

Not all memes are bad, particularly when they are used as a marketing strategy. In 2023, the average time spent per day on social media worldwide amounted to 151 minutes.[27] This gives marketers a strong reason to create content which consumers can identify with and to use platforms which are frequented by consumers. Netflix has been known for its innovative and engaging marketing strategies, and its use of memes is no exception. The company has effectively used memes to promote their content and engage with their audience on social media. Here are a few ways in which Netflix has used memes as part of their marketing strategy:[28]

1. **Using trending memes:** Netflix is always up-to-date with the latest trending memes and uses them to promote their content. For example, they used the

'Distracted Boyfriend' meme to promote their show 'Stranger Things'.

2. **Creating their own memes:** Netflix also creates their own memes related to its content, which can be funny and relatable. They use these memes to create buzz around their shows and movies and to engage with their audience.

3. **Partnering with meme creators:** Netflix has also partnered with popular meme creators to promote their content. For example, they collaborated with the Instagram account 'The Boys Club' to promote the show 'The Umbrella Academy'.

4. **Engaging with fans:** Netflix is known for engaging with its fans on social media, and memes are a great way to do that. They often reply to fans' comments with funny memes related to their content.

Netflix's meme marketing strategy is all about being relevant, relatable and engaging with their audience. By using memes, they can promote their content in a fun and creative way while also building a connection with their fans. Therefore, memes can be used as a positive marketing strategy, and many brands and companies are using them effectively to engage with their audience and promote their products or services. Here are some reasons why memes can be a positive marketing strategy:

1. **Memes are relatable:** Memes are often based on relatable situations, emotions and experiences, which

makes them an effective tool for connecting with the audience. By using memes, brands can show that they understand their customers and share their sense of humour.

2. **Memes can create buzz:** Memes have the potential to go viral, which can create a lot of buzz around a brand or product. If a meme is funny, clever or relatable enough, people will share it on social media, and it can quickly reach a large audience.

3. **Memes can be cost-effective:** Creating memes can be a cost-effective way to promote a brand or product. Unlike traditional advertising, which can be expensive, memes can be created quickly and easily, and they don't require a big budget.

4. **Memes can build brand awareness:** By using memes, brands can build brand awareness and establish their brand's personality. When people see a funny or clever meme, they are more likely to remember the brand behind it.

Memes have become a popular marketing strategy in recent years due to their ability to quickly capture the attention of a large audience and generate engagement. Using memes in brand marketing can help brands connect with their audience on a more personal level, increase brand awareness and create a positive brand image. Memes can also help brands create a more human persona, which can help build trust and credibility with their audience.

Here are some examples of memes used as a marketing strategy:

Wendy's Twitter account: Wendy's is known for using humour and memes on their Twitter account to engage with their followers. They frequently respond to tweets with witty and humorous comments, often using popular memes to convey their message.[29]

Old Spice commercials: Old Spice is a brand that has become known for its humorous and viral commercials that often include memes and internet culture references. Their 'The Man Your Man Could Smell Like' campaign is a great example of using memes and humour to create a memorable and shareable marketing campaign.[30]

Denny's Tumblr account: Denny's Tumblr account is another example of a brand using memes to connect with its audience. They often post humorous memes and images related to food and pop culture, which helps to create a fun and engaging social media presence.[31]

Ryan Reynolds' Aviation Gin commercials: Ryan Reynolds is known for his humorous and irreverent personality, and he brought that same energy to his marketing campaign for Aviation Gin. His commercials often included memes and pop culture references, and helped to create a viral buzz around the brand.[32]

Apple's 'What's a Computer?': This ad by Apple is a great example of a brand using a meme to create a memorable and impactful marketing campaign. The ad features a young girl using an iPad Pro and responding to a neighbour's question about what she's doing with the device. Her response, 'What's a computer?' became a popular meme on social media and helped to promote the iPad Pro as a modern and versatile device.[33]

Here are a few examples of how brands in India have used memes as a marketing strategy:

Zomato: Zomato, an Indian food delivery platform, has used memes to engage with its target audience on social media. They have created memes that are relevant to food and dining, such as 'When you order food and it arrives on time' or 'When the delivery boy forgets the chutney'.[34]

Swiggy: Swiggy, another Indian food delivery platform, has also used memes to connect with its audience. They have created humorous memes related to food and delivery, such as 'When the delivery boy comes early' or 'When you order food for one and end up eating for two.'[35]

Amul: Amul, a popular Indian dairy brand, has been using memes as a marketing strategy for years. They have created memes related to current events or pop culture and added their own witty captions, such as 'Aamchi

Mumbai, Aamchi Mumbai' during the Mumbai floods or 'Butterly Delicious' during the release of the movie *Padmaavat*.[36]

Netflix: Netflix India has also used memes to promote their shows and movies. They have created memes based on popular Indian characters or situations and added captions related to their content, such as *Chhalaang kaafi hai* for the release of the movie *Chhalaang*.[37]

These are just a few examples of how memes have been used as a marketing strategy in India. The use of memes allows brands to connect with their audience in a more relatable and humorous way, which can increase engagement and brand loyalty. Memes have become a ubiquitous part of internet culture and have evolved over time, becoming more complex and nuanced. With the increasing use of social media and the internet, memes are likely to continue to be an important way for people to express themselves and communicate with each other. However, it's important for brands to use memes in a way that is appropriate and relevant to their target audience. Memes can be a tricky area to navigate, and using them in wrong ways can backfire and harm a brand's reputation. So, it's essential for brands to do their research and ensure that they understand the culture and context behind the memes they plan to use.

Memes have been used as a tool for brands to compete against each other in the marketplace. This strategy is called 'memetic marketing' or 'memejacking', and it involves leveraging existing memes to create new content that promotes a brand or product. For example, in 2019, Burger King released a series of memes mocking McDonald's and their Happy Meal toys. Burger King's campaign was called Real Meals, and it aimed to promote the idea that people's emotions are more complex than just being 'happy' all the time.[38] Burger King used memes to create funny and relatable content that resonated with their target audience while also taking a jab at their competitor. Similarly, in 2020, PepsiCo released a meme-inspired commercial (inspired by the movie 'The Shining' starring Jack Nicholson) for its Mountain Dew Zero Sugar product featuring the character 'Count Zero' competing against Coca-Cola's Coke Zero Sugar. The commercial used a variety of memes, including the 'Surprised Pikachu' meme and the 'But That's None of My Business' meme, to create a humorous and engaging ad that appealed to a younger audience.[39] However, brands need to be careful when using memes in their marketing campaigns against competitors. Memes can be a double-edged sword, and if not executed properly, they can come across as inappropriate or offensive. Brands must ensure that they are not crossing any lines or harming their competitors' reputation while using memes to compete.

Memes Are Here to Stay

Memes have become a fundamental aspect of our online culture, and their popularity has only grown in recent years.

They provide a quick and often humorous way to convey information and opinions, and they have become a form of social commentary and political satire.

As technology continues to advance, we can expect that memes will evolve as well. One potential avenue is the use of augmented reality and virtual reality, which could allow for even more immersive and interactive memes.

Another possibility is that memes may become even more politically charged and used as a tool for activism and social justice movements. With the increasing prevalence of social media platforms and the ability to share content globally, memes have the potential to reach millions of people and have a significant impact.

However, there is also a risk that the use of memes could become more polarizing and divisive. In recent years, there have been concerns about the spread of misinformation and hate speech through memes. As a result, it is important to consider the ethics of meme creation and distribution.

One possible direction for the future of memes is that they may become more personalized and targeted. As AI and machine-learning technologies advance, it's possible that memes will be generated and tailored to individual preferences based on data analysis of user behaviour and interests.[40] This could lead to a more personalized and engaging experience for users. Another possibility is that memes will become more integrated with virtual and augmented reality technologies, creating immersive and interactive experiences. With the rise of VR and AR, it's possible that users will be able to interact with memes in new and exciting ways, allowing them to fully immerse themselves in the meme culture.[41] It's important to note that the evolution of memes will continue to be influenced by cultural and societal trends. As new ideas and issues emerge, memes will likely continue to reflect and comment on them in creative and unexpected ways.

VI

Role of Media in Spreading Fake News

'The greatest monster that there is: fake news media: torture with bullying, psychological warfare, spying and then using truthful misleading to complete their plot. The cheapest job ever.'

—Maria Karvouni

In 2020, AajTak was accused of spreading fake news claiming that the Indian movie star Sushant Singh Rajput had posted three tweets stating his intention to end his life just hours before his death. Similarly, in 2020, Zee News was accused of spreading fake news about the Tablighi Jamaat[1] event in Delhi, alleging its connection to the spread of COVID-19 in India.[2]

Not just Indian media outlets, but also those in the US have faced similar accusations of spreading fake news. In 2020, Fox News was sued for $2.7 billion for spreading false information about the 2020 US presidential election.[3]

The lawsuit claimed that the network had misled its viewers by promoting false claims about the election. In another case, the BBC apologized for airing a report in 2020 that contained false claims about the use of chemical weapons in Syria.[4] The report was based on a source that was later found to be unreliable. These are just a few examples, and there have been several other instances where news channels have been accused of spreading fake news, either deliberately or without doing due diligence. It is important to verify the authenticity of any news before disseminating it. It is important to note that while there have been instances of news channels spreading fake news, not all news channels engage in this behaviour. It is important to be vigilant and fact-check information before accepting it as true.

So, Does the Media Manipulate Millions?

The mainstream media plays an important role in informing the public about important events and issues. Unfortunately, they have also been known to spread fake news. The role of the mainstream media in spreading fake news can vary depending on the situation, but here are a few possible ways it can happen:

Rushing to be the first to report: In the race to be the first to break a story, some journalists and media outlets may not take the time to verify information, which can lead to the spread of fake news. The media landscape is highly competitive, and many news outlets strive to be the first to break a story or provide exclusive information. However, this zeal can sometimes lead to mistakes or inaccuracies in reporting. In recent years, the phenomenon of fake news has become a major concern, with some media outlets deliberately spreading false information to gain clicks and views. This has led to increased scrutiny of the media and calls for more responsible reporting.

It is important for journalists and news organizations to prioritize accuracy and fact-checking over speed when reporting on breaking news. While being the first to report can be important, it should not come at the cost of accuracy or the public's trust in the media.

Confirmation bias: We have discussed confirmation bias in detail in the previous chapters. Journalists, like everyone else, may be more likely to believe information that fits their preconceived notions or biases, and they may be less likely to fact-check information that confirms their beliefs. Journalists, like all human beings, can have preconceived notions or biases that may influence their reporting. These biases can come from a variety of sources, including personal experiences, cultural backgrounds, political affiliations and more. When journalists encounter information that aligns with their pre-existing beliefs or biases, they may be more likely to accept it without critically examining its accuracy or veracity. Moreover, with big-ticket investments in media houses and government influence in editorial decision-making, the situation is more complicated than it seems.

This phenomenon is sometimes referred to as confirmation bias, which is the tendency to seek out and accept information that confirms one's existing beliefs while ignoring or dismissing information that contradicts them. Confirmation bias can lead to a lack of objectivity in reporting and can ultimately harm the credibility of the journalist and the media outlet they work for. To combat confirmation bias, it is important for journalists to actively seek out diverse perspectives and viewpoints, challenge their own assumptions, and critically evaluate the information they receive. Journalists can also benefit from diverse newsroom environments and constructive feedback from colleagues to help them recognize and address any potential biases they may hold.

Lack of fact-checking: In some cases, media outlets may not have adequate fact-checking processes in place, or they may rely on unreliable sources. The lack of fact-checking by media channels on fake information can have serious consequences. In today's age of rapid information dissemination through social media, false information can spread quickly and cause harm. If the media fails to fact-check and disseminate false information, it can add credibility to false narratives and cause confusion among the public. One of the consequences of this is that people may make decisions based on false information. For example, during the COVID-19 pandemic, false information about cures, treatments and prevention methods was widespread on social media. This caused people to make uninformed decisions about their health and well-being, which could have been dangerous in some cases.

Another consequence is that it can erode trust in the media. If people feel that they cannot rely on mainstream media to provide accurate information, they may turn to alternative sources that may be less credible or even dangerous. This can lead to further polarization and confusion in society.

To address this issue, media channels should prioritize fact-checking and ensure that the information they disseminate is accurate and reliable. This can be done through rigorous editorial processes, partnerships with fact-checking organizations and transparency about sources and methods. Additionally, media literacy programmes can help educate the public on how to identify false information and rely on credible sources.

Sensationalism: Sensationalism in media reporting refers to the use of exaggeration, sensational language and other tactics to make a story more exciting or attention-grabbing, often at the expense of accuracy or objectivity. Media outlets may prioritize stories that are sensational or attention-grabbing, even if they are not entirely accurate. This can lead to the spread of false or misleading information. Media outlets may prioritize stories that are sensational, eye-catching or controversial in order to attract attention and generate more traffic or revenue. Unfortunately, this can sometimes lead to the spread of misinformation or inaccurate reporting, as journalists or media companies may prioritize getting clicks or views over ensuring the accuracy and reliability of their reporting. It is important for consumers of media to be critical and discerning when consuming news and information, and to seek out reliable sources and fact-checking resources in order to verify the accuracy of stories that they come across. Additionally, it is important for media companies and journalists to prioritize accuracy and responsible reporting in their work, in order to maintain public trust and credibility in the media. It is important to note that sensationalizing news is not limited to just one media channel or country, and can happen in any form of media. However, here are a few examples of media channels in India as well as abroad that have been accused of sensationalizing news:

1. **Republic TV:** Republic TV is a news channel known for its aggressive reporting style and sensationalist coverage of news. The channel has been criticized for its coverage of the Sushant Singh Rajput case, where it was accused of conducting a media trial and spreading baseless conspiracy theories.[5]

2. **Times Now:** Times Now is another news channel that has been accused of sensationalizing news. The channel has been criticized for its coverage of the JNU sedition case, where it was accused of running a trial by the media and spreading false information.[6]

3. **Zee News:** Zee News is a popular news channel in India which has also been accused of sensationalizing news. The channel has been criticized for its coverage

of the Delhi riots in 2020, where it was accused of spreading communal hatred and inciting violence.[7]

4. **Daily Mail:** The Daily Mail, a British tabloid newspaper, is often criticized for sensationalizing news stories. It is known for its sensational headlines and controversial articles.[8]

5. **Fox News:** Fox News, a conservative news network in the United States, has been accused of sensationalizing news stories in order to push a political agenda. The network has been criticized for its coverage of issues like immigration, crime and terrorism.[9]

6. **The Sun:** The Sun is a British tabloid that has been criticized for sensationalizing news stories. It has been accused of publishing misleading or inaccurate headlines and stories in order to sell more newspapers.[10]

7. **BuzzFeed:** BuzzFeed is a digital media company that has been accused of sensationalizing news stories in order to generate clicks and views. The company has been criticized for publishing misleading or inaccurate stories in order to drive traffic to its website.[11]

These are just a few examples, and it is important to note that sensationalism can occur in media outlets regardless of political affiliation or country of origin. A specific example of such sensationalism of news is the article published by Notallowedto.com under the headline 'Donald Trump Caught Snorting Cocaine by Hotel Staff',[12] with no byline or date of publication. According to this article, Maria Gonzalez, an employee of the hotel

Folks Inn & Suites Hotel, had witnessed it all. The article quoted her as saying,

> When I walked in, I saw 3 bimbos and maybe 100,000 in hundred dollars bills and a mountain of white powder on the table, I thought it was a dog on the floor sleep but it was his hair piece, he was bald and sweating like crazy. I asked him where to put the food and he asked me did I wanna take a hit, I told him no, he called me a freeloader, told me to get the fuck out his room and go back to my country.

When the media approached Trump's team for a reaction, they released a statement saying, 'I did not disrespect that woman. She's a liar, and I don't do drugs, I do business. When I get elected, all hotel employees will have to be US citizens. They keep taking real American people's jobs and that will stop, not on my watch.' The website subsequently attracted a lot of traffic based on the sensational fake story, but very few people believed it. Again, this was the US, which has a high literacy rate and digital awareness. Had such an incident played out in India, the impact would have been much different.

Clickbait headlines: 'You won't believe what happened next!' or 'The shocking truth about XYZ!' Such headlines are designed to entice readers to click on a story without providing any real information. While clickbait headlines can be effective in driving traffic to a website, they can also be misleading and manipulative. Some media outlets have faced criticism for using clickbait to generate revenue at the expense of accuracy and responsible journalism.

Clickbait headlines are a common practice in many countries, including India. Some examples of Indian media channels using clickbait headlines in the past include:

1. 'Shocking! Salman Khan Caught Drunk-Driving Again!'—this headline was used by a popular Indian entertainment news website to attract readers to an article about the actor being involved in a car accident.[13]
2. 'Shocking secrets about Deepika Padukone'—this headline was used by a tabloid-style YouTube channel to attract readers to a video about the actress's unknown facts about her professional and personal life.[14]
3. '10 Bollywood Celebrities Who Are Unrecognizable Without Makeup'—this headline was used by a lifestyle YouTube channel to attract readers to a video featuring photos of celebrities without makeup.[15]

These are just a few examples, and it is important to note that not all media channels use clickbait headlines. However, clickbait has become a widespread practice in the media industry, as it attracts more clicks and engagement from readers, which ultimately translates into revenue for the website.

Overhyping stories: News outlets may exaggerate the importance or significance of a story to generate more interest. For example, a minor car accident may be reported as a major traffic disaster.

Using emotional language: Some news outlets use emotive language to make a story more dramatic. For example, a story about a political scandal might use words like 'explosive', 'shocking', or 'outrageous' to describe the situation.

Sensational images: News outlets may use graphic or shocking images to grab readers' attention. For example, a story about a natural disaster might feature a photo of a devastated community, even if the photo is not directly related to the story.

Biased reporting: Some news outlets may use sensationalism to advance a particular agenda or political viewpoint. They may present facts in a way that supports their position or ignore information that contradicts it.

Sensationalism in media reporting can lead to distorted perceptions of reality and contribute to the spread of misinformation. It is important to be critical of the information presented in news stories and to seek out multiple sources to get a more accurate picture of events.

The Media Circus

Though there are many who are well-informed about current events and research various sources to seek and validate information, some corporate-funded, insensitive and powerful media outlets go to great lengths to manipulate and influence their minds. Unfortunately, many people's media consumption relies on shallow mediums like WhatsApp and other social media channels, where the information they consume can be likened to junk food for their minds. Excessive screen time, mindless content and sensationalized news contribute to a decline in critical thinking and intelligence.

TV news channels, in their race for Television Rating Points (TRPs), have devolved into entertainment outlets with animated videos, ticker crawlers, cacophonous debates and dramatic soundtracks, and have turned themselves into platforms for media trials.

Every small event is sensationalized and covered by every channel and repeated without any incremental content again and again throughout the day. Such a situation is best described as a 'media circus', which refers to a situation where the media is excessively focused on a particular event, story or person, often to the point of sensationalizing the coverage and creating a frenzy of attention. This can happen with high-profile court cases, political scandals, celebrity controversies or other events that capture the public's interest. The media circus can have both positive and negative effects. On one hand, it can help shed light on important issues and bring attention to stories that might otherwise be overlooked. It can also provide a platform for victims to speak out and for important voices to be heard.

On the other hand, the media circus can also be detrimental. It can create a distorted and sensationalized view of events, perpetuate misinformation and lead to unfair treatment of the parties involved. It can also be overwhelming and intrusive, making it difficult for those involved to deal with the situation in a calm and measured way. The media circus is a complex phenomenon that can have both positive and negative impacts, and it is important for media outlets to be mindful of their responsibility to report accurately and ethically. There are many incidents that turned into media circuses, such as the death of actor Sushant Singh Rajput, the Nirbhaya case, the IPL spot-fixing scandal in 2012, the Aarushi Talwar murder in 2008, the Sunanda Pushkar death, Princess Diana's fatal crash and the trial of NFL player O.J. Simpson.

A media circus can sometimes lead to the spread of fake news and misinformation, as journalists may be more interested in getting a scoop than in the verification of information. This style of journalism has drawn both praise and criticism from different quarters. Some view an aggressive approach as a refreshing departure from the more staid and conventional style of news reporting, while others criticize it for promoting a polarizing and confrontational approach that can be counterproductive to reasoned debate and dialogue.

The impact of a media circus on people can be significant and can manifest in several ways:

1. **Emotional response:** People may become emotionally invested in a media circus, feeling anger, fear or

outrage over the coverage of the event. This can lead to heightened levels of stress, anxiety and frustration.

2. **Perception of reality:** The media circus can shape people's perceptions of reality, often by exaggerating or sensationalizing events. This can lead to confusion and misinformation about the facts surrounding the event.

3. **Bias:** The media circus can also reflect and reinforce existing biases, leading to further polarization and division among people.

4. **Distraction:** The media circus can distract people from other important issues or events that may be happening simultaneously. This can lead to a lack of focus and attention on critical issues that require public awareness and action.

5. **Desensitization:** In some cases, the media circus can lead to desensitization, where people become numb to the event's impact or severity due to the constant and often overwhelming coverage.

The impact of a media circus on people can be complex and multifaceted, with both positive and negative consequences. It is important for individuals to critically evaluate media coverage and seek out reliable sources of information to avoid being overwhelmed or misinformed.

In today's digital age, the spread of fake news and media circuses has become a major concern. It is important for people to be vigilant and to fact-check information before believing or sharing it. It is also important for media organizations to prioritize accuracy and ethics in their reporting, and to resist the temptation to engage in sensationalism and hype.

The Power of Media Propaganda

Media propaganda refers to the dissemination of information, whether accurate or not, through various media channels in order to manipulate public opinion or promote a certain agenda. The power of media propaganda lies in its ability to influence how people think, feel and behave.

One of the main reasons media propaganda is so powerful is that it can reach a large audience very quickly through various mediums such as television, radio, newspapers, social media and other online platforms. By using emotional language, powerful imagery and persuasive messaging, propaganda can evoke strong emotional responses in people, which can then shape their attitudes and beliefs. Another reason media propaganda is so powerful is that it can be difficult to distinguish between accurate and biased information. In some cases, propaganda may be disguised as legitimate news or factual information, which can make it even more difficult for people to critically evaluate the information they are receiving.

In addition, media propaganda often plays on people's fears, prejudices and biases, which can make it even more effective in influencing public opinion. By tapping into these emotional triggers, propaganda can create a sense of urgency or a need for action, which can then motivate people to support a particular cause or political agenda.

Edward Bernays, nephew of Sigmund Freud, also known as the 'Father of Public Relations', wrote books like *Crystallizing Public Opinion* and *Propaganda*[16] which derived literature from social science and psychology manipulations to build theory on influencing and shaping public opinion through media. He has been instrumental in creating the perception that smoking cigarettes is glamorous. Hired by the American Tobacco Company, Bernays hired a group of beautiful women and had them walk in New York City's Easter Parade while smoking cigarettes. He then released a press note claiming these women lit the 'Torches of Freedom' in an act of reclamation of women's rights as it was still taboo for women to smoke cigarettes. The *New York Times* carried this story with the headline, 'Group of Girls Puff at Cigarettes as a Gesture of Freedom'. Bernays was thus able to develop a marketing strategy with which he manipulated the media to link it to the women's rights movement.

Similarly, Bernays was hired by the De Beers diamond company to boost the demand for diamonds. In the 1930s, diamonds were not commonly used in engagement rings, and the market for diamonds was relatively small. De Beers tasked Bernays with creating a marketing campaign to boost demand for diamonds. He then launched a highly successful campaign that linked diamonds with love and marriage.

Bernays started by targeting the influential and wealthy, who would then set the trend for the rest of society. He placed stories about diamond engagement rings in popular magazines and newspapers, highlighting the romantic and sentimental nature of diamonds. He also arranged for Hollywood celebrities to be seen wearing diamonds, further promoting their desirability.

The campaign was highly effective, and by the end of the 1930s, the sale of diamonds had increased by 50 per cent. The De Beers company had successfully created a new cultural norm that linked diamonds with love and commitment, and the diamond engagement ring became a symbol of enduring love.

Today, the diamond engagement ring remains one of the most popular symbols of love and marriage, thanks in part to Edward Bernays' innovative marketing campaign. In his book *Propaganda*,[17] Bernays says, 'The conscious and intelligent manipulation of the organized habits and opinions of the masses is an important element in a democratic society. Those who manipulate this unseen mechanism of society constitute an invisible government which is the true ruling power of our country . . . We are governed, our minds are moulded, our tastes formed, our ideas suggested, largely by men we have never heard of. This is a logical result of the way in which our democratic society is organized. Vast numbers of human beings must cooperate in this manner if they are to live together as a smoothly functioning society . . . In almost every act of our daily lives, whether in the sphere of politics or business, in our social conduct or our ethical thinking, we are dominated by the relatively small number of persons . . . who understand the mental processes and social patterns of the masses. It is they who pull the wires which control the public mind.'[18]

Late-Night Talk Show as a Medium to Spread Propaganda

Late-night talk shows are primarily designed for entertainment, but they can also be used to spread propaganda if the host or producers have a specific agenda. However, it's important to note that mainstream late-night talk shows have a large and diverse audience, so it can be difficult to spread propaganda without raising suspicion. If a host or producers were to use a late-night talk show as a medium to spread propaganda, they would likely use techniques such as selective reporting, cherry-picking information or presenting biased opinions as facts. They may also use humour or satire to make their propaganda more palatable to the audience.

Jimmy Fallon replaced Jay Leno in 2014 as the *Tonight Show* host after Leno was fired by NBC for going too hard on President Barack Obama.[19] Though Obama was the butt of many jokes, it was Leno who took off his gloves and targeted Obama left, right and centre. Fallon was also under pressure after he invited Donald Trump on his talk show and went soft on him. So, the producer wanted Fallon to 'go political' and bash Trump through his jokes as the viewers were looking for an anti-Trump theme on the show.[20] But more was yet to come, when Stephen Colbert replaced David Letterman on *Late Show* in 2015. He was so hard on Trump that it became an obsession. People joked that Colbert could deliver an anti-Trump monologue for the duration of an entire show and the *New York Post* even ran a story on how he was promoting the Democrat agenda. In many other countries, the media does not have such freedom of expression, so not many examples can be drawn. It's important to stay vigilant and critical of the information presented on any media platform, including late-night talk shows. By fact-checking and researching the information presented, audiences can avoid being misled by propaganda.

Setting the Agenda

Agenda setting by the media refers to the power of the media to influence which topics are considered important and which are not. This concept suggests that the media has the ability to shape public opinion and determine which issues receive attention from policymakers and the general public. In other words, the media agenda setting theory argues that the media does not tell people what to think, but rather what to think about. The media can shape the public's perception of important issues by choosing which stories to cover, how to cover them and how prominently to feature them. By focusing on certain topics and ignoring others, the media can create a particular agenda that can influence public opinion and policy decisions.

For example, if the media gives significant coverage to a particular social issue, such as climate change, it can increase public awareness of the issue and encourage policymakers to take action. Conversely, if the media does not give much attention to an issue, it may be seen as less important by the public and policymakers, even if it is a critical issue that requires attention.

This theory suggests that the media plays a powerful role in shaping public discourse and influencing the political agenda. Media has been setting the agenda for many issues such as the coverage of the 2020 US presidential election, coverage on climate change, COVID-19, gun control, etc. In India, the media seems to be more biased in setting of the agenda, whether it is the 2019 Lok Sabha elections, the farmers' protest of 2020-21 or the drug scandal that rocked the Hindi film industry in 2020. Also, the media projects certain topics and tries to influence how they are perceived. They can influence the direction of a debate by selecting panellists of their choice, asking pointed questions and influencing public perception.

Lies by Omission

Not only does the media set the agenda for discussion on topics of national interest, but it can also engage in 'Lies by Omission' by intentionally leaving out important facts or information to shape the perception of the audience in a particular way.

This can involve leaving out information that contradicts a particular viewpoint, failing to provide context that would give a different perspective or ignoring relevant information that would challenge a particular narrative.

Media engaging in lying by omission can be particularly insidious because it is not always immediately apparent to the audience that information is being left out. It can also be difficult to detect because it requires a deep understanding of the topic at hand and the ability to identify what information is missing. However, it is important to note that not all omissions of information are intentional. Journalists and news organizations also omit information unintentionally due to factors such as limited time, resources or access to information. So how does the media lie by omission? Here are some ways the media can lie by omission:

1. **Selective editing of video footage:** When a media outlet selectively edits video footage to convey a certain narrative, it can be considered a lie by omission. For example, if a news organization shows only a small portion of a protest where violence breaks out, without showing the peaceful nature of the rest of the protest, it can create a misleading impression of the event.

2. **Ignoring important details:** If a media outlet chooses to ignore important details of a story, it can be a lie by omission. For example, if a news story reports that a political candidate was caught in a scandal but fails to mention that the allegations were later proven false, the omission can mislead readers and viewers.

3. **Failing to report on certain events:** If a media outlet chooses not to report on certain events, it can be a lie by

omission. For example, if a news outlet chooses not to cover a protest or rally, it can give the impression that the event did not happen or was not significant.

4. **Biased reporting:** If a media outlet consistently reports only one side of a story, it can be considered a lie by omission. For example, if a news organization only reports on the negative actions of one political party, while ignoring the misdeeds of another, it can create a misleading impression of the political landscape.

5. **Using misleading headlines:** If a media outlet uses a misleading headline that does not accurately reflect the content of the story, it can be considered a lie by omission. For example, if a news organization publishes a headline stating that a political candidate was caught in a scandal, but the story only mentions minor infractions, it can mislead readers and viewers.

In the lead-up to the Iraq War, many media outlets, including the *New York Times*, reported that Iraq possessed weapons of mass destruction (WMDs)[21] based on intelligence reports. However, they failed to question the validity of the reports or investigate further, leading to a false narrative that helped justify the war. Also, some media outlets have been accused of downplaying the severity of climate change by omitting or understating key facts and data. For example, in 2017, Fox News[22] aired a segment claiming that global temperatures had not increased in the past twenty years, which was quickly debunked by climate scientists who pointed out that the segment used a selectively chosen timeframe that excluded the hottest years on record.

Here are some examples of media lying by omission in India:

1. **Coverage of the 2002 Gujarat riots:** The mainstream media in India was accused of lying by omission in its coverage of the 2002 Gujarat riots. Many news outlets failed to report on the role of the state government and its leaders in the violence and instead focused on the communal tensions between Hindus and Muslims.

2. **Coverage of the Kashmir conflict:** The Indian media has been accused of lying by omission in its coverage of the Kashmir conflict. Many news outlets have failed to report on human rights violations committed by the Indian security forces and instead portrayed the conflict as a battle between India and Pakistan.

3. **Coverage of the Hathras rape case:** In 2020, a Dalit woman was allegedly gang-raped in Hathras, Uttar Pradesh. The Indian media was accused of lying by omission in its coverage of the case. Many news outlets failed to report on the caste-based violence and discrimination that led to the incident.

4. **Coverage of the Delhi riots:** In 2020, communal violence broke out in northeast Delhi. The Indian media was accused of lying by omission in its coverage

of the riots. Many news outlets failed to report on the role of politicians and police officers in instigating the violence and instead focused on the clashes between Hindus and Muslims.

5. **Coverage of the farmers' protest:** In 2020–21, farmers in India protested the new agricultural laws introduced by the government. The Indian media was accused of lying by omission in its coverage of the protests. Many news outlets failed to report on the concerns of the farmers and instead portrayed the protests as anti-national and anti-government.

Fake News and the Power of Social Media

It is essential to critically evaluate news sources and their reporting by the media news channels to ensure that the information presented is accurate, comprehensive and unbiased. The Indian media landscape includes over 900 TV channels and 1000 radio stations telecasting programmes in English, Hindi and many other regional languages.[23] It is dominated by TV and newspapers and more viewers or readers coming from the Hindi segment with AajTak and TVNews18 commanding the largest share of viewership. On the trust factor, it is the *Times of India* which is considered the most trusted news brand. Also, with rapid penetration of the Internet and smartphones and around 600 million netizens active on social media, the sources of news consumption are changing drastically.

Share of sources used to access news across India in 2022

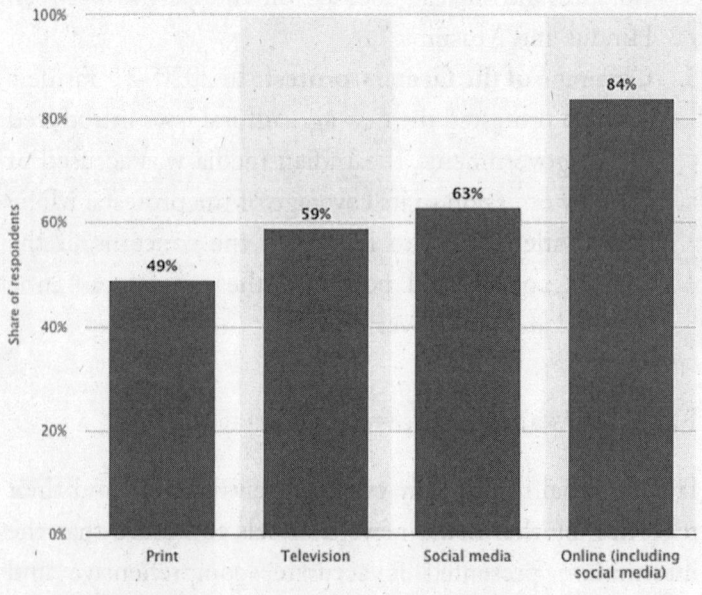

Source: Statista 2023

Since more and more people are relying on social media to consume news, social media has played a significant role in the rapid spread of fake news in recent years. With the rise of platforms like Facebook, Twitter, Instagram and TikTok, it has become easier for false information to be shared and amplified quickly. One of the main reasons why social media has contributed to the spread of fake news is the ease of sharing information. With just a few clicks, anyone can share a post or article with their followers, who can then share it with their followers, and so on. This means that false information can quickly go viral, even if it is not based on facts or evidence. Another reason why social media has facilitated the spread of fake news is the way that the algorithms work. These algorithms are designed to show users content that they are likely to engage with, based on their past behaviour on the platform. This means that if someone has engaged with fake news in the past, they are more likely to be shown similar content in the future. This creates a cycle where false information is continually being shared and amplified.

Social media has made it easier for individuals and organizations to create and disseminate fake news. Anyone can create a website or social media account and start sharing false information, often with little to no oversight. This has allowed conspiracy theorists, political operatives and others to spread misinformation and propaganda with ease. The role of social media in spreading fake news cannot be overstated. While these platforms have many benefits, they have also created an environment where false information can thrive, often with serious consequences for individuals and society as a whole.

Though social media platforms like Facebook and Twitter have taken steps to curb the spread of fake news, questions remain about their outcome. Some of the steps taken by social media to curb fake news include:

1. **Fact-checking:** Social media platforms have partnered with fact-checking organizations to verify the accuracy

of news articles and posts before they are published on their platforms.

2. **Warning labels:** Social media platforms have started adding warning labels to content that has been flagged as potentially false or misleading. These warning labels inform users that the content they are about to read may not be accurate.

3. **Algorithm changes:** Social media platforms have updated their algorithms to prioritize content from trusted sources and reduce the visibility of posts containing false information.

4. **Removing content:** Social media platforms have been removing content that violates their policies regarding the spread of misinformation.

5. **Reporting tools:** Social media platforms have introduced reporting tools that allow users to flag content that they believe to be false or misleading.

6. **Education campaigns:** Social media platforms have launched campaigns to educate users on how to identify fake news and how to report it.

7. **Third-party partnerships:** Social media platforms have partnered with academic institutions, non-governmental organizations and other stakeholders to develop solutions to tackle fake news.

Facebook's transparency centre says, 'Reducing the spread of false news on Facebook is a responsibility that we take seriously. We also recognize that this is a challenging and sensitive issue. We want to help people stay informed without stifling productive public discourse. There is also a fine line between false news and satire or opinion.'[24]

If a story is flagged as false, Facebook reduces its distribution in the news feed and adds a warning label. Also, Facebook has made updates to its news feed algorithm to prioritize content from trusted sources and to reduce the visibility of sensationalist and clickbait headlines. Further, it has taken steps to disrupt financial incentives for spammers and fake news creators, such as by banning certain types of ads or limiting the monetization options for pages that are found to repeatedly share false information.

On the other hand, the Twitter help centre's guidelines on 'misleading media' read, 'You may not share synthetic, manipulated, or out-of-context media that may deceive or confuse people and lead to harm ('misleading media'). In addition, we may label tweets containing misleading media to help people understand their authenticity and to provide additional context.'[25]

If Twitter finds anyone violating the policy, including images, videos, audios, gifs, and URLs hosting relevant content, it will label or remove it.

Though both mainstream and social media are taking steps to curb fake news on their platforms, there's still a long way to go. Fake news articles got six times more clicks on Facebook than actual news during the 2020 presidential elections in the US. Research has proved that Facebook is far ahead of other platforms like Google, Twitter etc. in the spread of fake news.

The rise of artificial intelligence and machine learning algorithms will hopefully detect and flag misinformation. Social media platforms are already using AI to identify and remove false or misleading content, and these technologies are likely to become more sophisticated and effective in the future. But again, it is not only the media's responsibility but also that of the citizens to safeguard themselves against misleading information. They can take the help of technology or approaches that make it easier for users to verify the accuracy of the information they encounter on social media. For example, some start-ups are developing browser extensions and other tools that can analyse the credibility of online sources and provide users with real-time feedback on the reliability of the information they are reading.

Finally, the fight against fake news in media will likely require a combination of technological innovation, public education and awareness, and policy interventions to address the root causes of misinformation and disinformation.

VII

Fake News Amplification

'We found that falsehood diffuses significantly farther, faster, deeper, and more broadly than the truth, in all categories of information, and in many cases by an order of magnitude.'

—Sinan Aral, professor at
MIT Sloan School of Management

Print and television media are battling for relevance in the age of digital media. There was a time when people would wake up early in the morning and wait for the paperboy to bring them news from around the world to their doorstep. Newspapers back then would keep the reader abreast of all major developments till the time of going to print, which would be roughly a few hours before being delivered to the reader. Television news has greatly reduced the amount of time it takes for news to reach us, but it still takes a couple of hours even for a 'breaking news' item to reach viewers. On the other hand, digital media functions almost on a real-time basis. For example, if India wins the World Cup, the news will first appear in digital media, then on television (unless we have live coverage) and in newspapers only the next day. The faster the news appears, the faster it is amplified on social media. Therefore, social media is responsible for faster and further amplification of news.

A 2018 study at the MIT Sloan School of Management found that fake news spreads faster on social media than real news.[1] The reason? Fake news is sensational and has a clear-cut target. This gives users an opportunity to use it to impose their point of view or confirmation bias. Fake news often plays on people's emotions and biases, which makes it more likely to go viral. People are more likely to share stories that make them angry, happy or afraid, without taking the time to fact-check them. Also, social media platforms make it easy for anyone to share information, without verifying whether it's true or not. This means that fake news can spread quickly before anyone has a chance to fact-check it.

Additionally, social media platforms offer users an escape from reality. Sigmund Freud observed that personal desires are always at odds with the realities of the world. Throughout our lives, we grapple with this conflict and as we grow up, we gradually come to terms with reality. However, our desire for pleasure persists and manifests in our interactions on social media. We tend to share interesting details about our lives, such as travel experiences, food choices, wardrobe purchases, who we are with and so on. We use social media to showcase our pleasurable desires separate from our day-to-day realities. We might feel envious of others' pleasurable experiences, such as their trip to Goa, and post our best pictures in a bid to stoke jealousy in them as well.

The fear of missing out (FOMO) drives much of our social media interactions and imagery. When we see others posting about fun events or experiences, it's natural to feel like we're missing out on something exciting. This feeling can lead us to engage more with social media, checking it more frequently and spending more time on it, in order to feel more connected to what's going on. Social media platforms are designed to be addictive, and they often use algorithms to show us content that is likely to keep us engaged. This can make it difficult to resist the urge to check our feeds, even if we know it's not necessarily productive or healthy for us. Also, social media can create a sense of social pressure to constantly be 'in the know' and up-to-date on the latest trends and events. This pressure can lead us to constantly check our feeds and engage with content, even if it's not something we're genuinely interested in.

FOMO is a phenomenon that refers to the feeling of anxiety or stress that can arise when individuals believe they are missing out on important events or experiences. In the context of social media and online news, FOMO can lead people to seek out and share news stories without fully verifying their accuracy or credibility, which can contribute to the spread of fake news. Fake news is often designed to appeal to people's emotions and exploit their fears, which can include the fear of missing out on important information or being left behind by others who are more informed. When individuals feel pressured to stay up-to-date with the latest news and information, they may be more likely to share stories without fact-checking them or considering their sources. This cognitive vulnerability can take many forms including FOMO. Here are a few examples of cognitive vulnerabilities of social media users:

1. **Confirmation Bias:** Social media users may be more likely to seek out information that confirms their existing beliefs or opinions. This can lead to a distorted view of reality and an inability to consider alternative perspectives.

2. **Availability Heuristic:** Social media users may rely heavily on information that is readily available to them on their feeds or from their social networks, without considering other sources of information. This can lead to a skewed perception of reality and an over-reliance on anecdotal evidence.

3. **Social Comparison:** Social media users may be more likely to compare themselves to others on their feeds, leading to feelings of inadequacy, jealousy or anxiety. This can lead to a negative self-image and a reduced sense of self-worth.

4. **FOMO:** Social media users may feel a sense of anxiety or stress when they perceive that they are missing out on social events or experiences. This can lead to compulsive

checking of social media feeds and a preoccupation with staying connected to social networks.

5. **Illusion of Control:** Social media users may feel a false sense of control over their online personas or the content they consume, leading to a tendency to overestimate their ability to shape their own online experiences. This can lead to a sense of disillusionment or frustration when they encounter content or interactions that are unexpected or unwanted.

Social media platforms have also contributed to the spread of fake news by creating an environment in which stories can be easily shared and amplified without proper vetting. In many cases, algorithms that prioritize engagement and virality over accuracy and credibility can exacerbate the problem by promoting sensational or misleading content. Spreading or sharing information on social media leads to its amplification as your friends, connections and followers might like, share or comment on your post and amplify its reach to their friends, connections and followers. Fake news amplification refers to the act of spreading false or misleading information to a larger audience through various means, such as social media, news outlets and other forms of digital communication. It involves the intentional spreading of disinformation or propaganda to shape public opinion, create confusion and manipulate people's beliefs and behaviour. Fake news amplification can have serious consequences for society, including undermining trust in the media, eroding democratic institutions, and inciting violence and social unrest. It is often used by political actors, special interest groups and other entities to push their agenda and achieve their objectives. One of the main reasons why fake news amplification is so effective is because it takes advantage of the way information spreads online. Social media algorithms, for example, tend to prioritize content that generates the most engagement, which can lead to false information spreading faster than accurate information. Additionally, people are often more likely to share information that confirms their existing beliefs, even if it is false.

Social media can amplify the spread of fake news in several ways. Here are some of the most common ways in which social media can amplify fake news:

1. **Viral Spread:** Social media allows fake news to spread quickly and easily. A single post or tweet can be shared and re-shared multiple times, potentially reaching millions of people within a short period of time.
2. **Echo Chambers:** Social media algorithms can create echo chambers, where people are only exposed to information that confirms their existing beliefs. This can make it easier for fake news to spread, as people are more likely to believe information that fits with their preconceived notions.
3. **Lack of Fact-Checking:** Many social media users do not fact-check the information they share. This means that fake news can be shared widely without anyone verifying its accuracy.

4. **Manipulation by Bad Actors:** Some bad actors intentionally create and spread fake news on social media for their own gain. This can include political propaganda or scams designed to trick people into giving away personal information or money.

Algorithmic Amplification[2]

Algorithmic amplification of fake news on social media is a phenomenon in which social media platforms' algorithms promote false or misleading content to a larger audience, leading to its viral spread. This happens when the algorithms of social media platforms, such as Facebook, Twitter, or YouTube, prioritize engagement metrics like shares, likes and comments over the accuracy and truthiness of the content. This algorithmic amplification of fake news on social media can have serious consequences, as false information can spread rapidly and cause harm. It can lead to misinformation and distrust in institutions, undermine democratic processes and even incite violence. Moreover, fake news can also be used as a tool for propaganda and disinformation campaigns by state actors or non-state actors, which can have serious geopolitical implications.

The flaws lie in the customer-centric designs of these social media platforms. These social media platforms are built around algorithms that study users' online activities and develop patterns to deliver content tailored to suit their preferences. They keep on delivering more of such content until the user is no longer able to distinguish between fake and real because of their confirmation bias. The main objective of social media is to maximise advertising revenue by exploiting the information collected from users' digital footprints and past activities. So, when you buy from Amazon, it recommends you to check out similar items. The same applies to Netflix or Facebook. This is done by a mathematical concept known as cosine similarity, which measures the similarity between two non-zero vectors in a high-dimensional space. It is often used in machine learning and natural language processing to compare the similarity between documents, words or user preferences. The cosine similarity measure calculates the cosine of the angle between two vectors, which can range from -1 to 1. The closer the cosine similarity value is to 1, the more similar the two vectors are, and the closer it is to -1, the more dissimilar they are. In recommendation systems, cosine similarity can be used to identify similar items or products based on their features. For example, if a user likes a particular movie on Netflix, the recommendation system can use the cosine similarity measure to find other movies with similar features such as genre, actors and plotlines. This allows the recommendation system to suggest new items that the user is likely to be interested in, based on their past preferences. Cosine similarity is particularly useful in recommendation systems that have a large number of features or dimensions, as it is able to effectively capture the similarities between items even in a high-dimensional space.

There are two types of recommender systems: content and collaborative.

Content-Based Recommender System

A content-based recommender system is a type of recommendation system that suggests items to a user based on the similarity between the content of the items and the user's preferences. Here's an example of how a content-based recommender system could work for recommending movies to a user:

1. The system first collects information about the user's movie preferences, such as genres, actors, directors and ratings of movies the user has already watched.
2. Next, the system collects information about the movies in its database, such as genre, actors, directors, plot summary and other relevant information.
3. Then, the system analyses the content of the movies and the user's preferences to identify the most relevant movies that match the user's interests.
4. Finally, the system generates a list of recommended movies for the user based on the content similarity between the movies and the user's preferences.

For example, if a user has a preference for action movies starring Tom Cruise, and has rated the *Mission Impossible* series highly, the system may recommend action movies starring Tom Cruise, such as *Top Gun* or *Jack Reacher*, based on the similarity of their content. The features used by content-based recommendation systems can include text descriptions, tags, images and other metadata associated with the items being recommended. These systems can also incorporate information about the user's demographics, such as age, gender and location, to tailor recommendations to their specific interests. One advantage of content-based recommendation systems is that they can provide recommendations for new or niche items that have not yet been rated by other users. However, they may struggle to capture the nuances of user preferences and may not be as effective as collaborative filtering in identifying serendipitous recommendations.

Collaborative Recommendation System

Collaborative Recommender Systems are a type of recommendation system that uses the preferences or feedback of a group of users to generate recommendations for individual users. In other words, these systems rely on the idea that users who have similar preferences or interests will like similar items. There are two main types of collaborative recommender systems: user-based and item-based.

User-based collaborative filtering involves finding users who have similar preferences to a given user and then recommending items that similar users have liked. Item-based collaborative filtering, on the other hand, involves finding items that are similar to the items that a user has liked and then recommending those similar items. Both types of collaborative filtering have their advantages and disadvantages. User-based filtering can be more effective when there are many users with similar preferences, while item-based filtering can be more effective when there are many items with similar attributes. Collaborative recommender systems are commonly used in online retail, music and video streaming platforms and social media websites, to suggest products or services that users may be interested in. These systems have also been used in research fields such as healthcare, where they can be used to recommend treatments or interventions based on the preferences and outcomes of similar patients. Here are some examples of Collaborative Recommender Systems:

1. **Netflix:** Netflix uses collaborative filtering to recommend movies and TV shows to its users based on their viewing history and the viewing history of other users who have similar tastes.[3]

2. **Amazon:** Amazon uses collaborative filtering to recommend products to its customers based on their purchase history and the purchase history of other customers who have similar preferences.[4]

3. **Spotify:** Spotify uses collaborative filtering to recommend songs and playlists to its users based on their listening history and the listening history of other users who have similar tastes.[5]

4. **Yelp:** Yelp uses collaborative filtering to recommend restaurants and other local businesses to its users based on their ratings and reviews and the ratings and reviews of other users who have similar preferences.[6]

5. **YouTube:** YouTube uses collaborative filtering to recommend videos to its users based on their viewing history and the viewing history of other users who have similar interests.[7]

Social media platforms are driven by algorithms that aim to increase user engagement and generate revenue through advertisements. So, can we have a digital environment where platforms do not try to earn money by manipulating our user behaviour and preferences? Maybe that is unlikely, as businesses exist to maximize profits. However, it is important to remember the Hindi adage—'सवारी अपने सामान की खुद जिम्मेवार है!' (Riders are responsible for their luggage).

One way users can identify the source of the content is by reaching the starting point of the thread and identifying how the information has travelled to them. This is called data provenance, which involves tracing and documenting the origin, ownership, custody and handling of data. On social media, data provenance is an important concept as it ensures the reliability and authenticity of the information shared online. Social media platforms like Facebook, Twitter and Instagram provide features that allow users to share content such as photos, videos and articles. However, not all content shared on social media is reliable or trustworthy as there is a significant risk of misinformation and fake news.

To ensure the accuracy and credibility of information shared on social media, data provenance techniques can be used. One way to establish data provenance is through metadata, which provides information about the origin and history of a piece of data. Metadata can include information such as the creation date, location and device used. This information can be used to verify the authenticity of the content and help identify the original source.

Digital signatures are another way to establish data provenance on social media. Digital signatures use encryption technology to verify the authenticity and integrity of a document or piece of content. This technique can be used to ensure that a post or message has not been tampered with and has been created by the intended author. Data provenance is a crucial concept in social media as it helps to establish the authenticity and reliability of information shared online. By using techniques such as metadata and digital signatures, users can ensure that the content they share and consume on social media is trustworthy and accurate.

All this might seem too technical for the average social media user. But while data provenance is typically used in professional contexts such as scientific research, it can also be useful for all. Here are a few practical ways in which a social media user can make use of data provenance:

1. **Check the source of information:** Before sharing or reposting information on social media, it is important to verify the source of the information. By looking at data provenance, you can check whether the information comes from a reliable and trustworthy source.

2. **Evaluate the credibility of content:** Understanding the history of a piece of content can help you evaluate its credibility. By looking at the data provenance, you can check whether the content has been edited, manipulated or taken out of context, which can affect its accuracy.

3. **Protect your privacy:** Social media platforms collect a lot of personal data about users, including their browsing history and interactions with other users. By understanding the data provenance of your personal information, you can take steps to protect your privacy and ensure that your data is not being misused or shared without your consent.

4. **Identify and report misinformation:** Social media is often used to spread misinformation and fake news. By understanding data provenance, you can identify misleading or false information and report it to the platform or other relevant authorities.

Do we do all this? Perhaps not. But it is important to keep in mind that data provenance can be a powerful tool for social media users who want to be more informed, responsible and secure online.

Bots and Propagation of Fake News[8]

Bots can play a significant role in the propagation of fake news. Bots are computer programs that can automate various tasks, including the dissemination of information on social media platforms. Bot networks can be used to spread false information rapidly and efficiently, creating the illusion of widespread support for a particular idea or viewpoint. Fake news is often spread through social media platforms such as Twitter and Facebook, where users can quickly share articles and posts with their followers. Bots can be programmed to retweet or share specific articles or posts, creating the appearance of widespread interest in a particular topic or idea. Here are a few examples of social media bots and the roles they play:

1. **Chatbots:** Interact with users in a chat interface, providing automated responses to users' messages.
2. **Spam bots:** Post large volumes of unsolicited content, often for promotional purposes.
3. **Malicious bots:** Engage in harmful activities, such as spreading malware or stealing personal information.
4. **Fake follower bots:** Follow and unfollow users in large numbers to artificially increase numbers.
5. **Content generation bots:** Generate and publish content automatically, such as news articles or social media posts.
6. **Influencer bots:** Mimic human influencers, posting sponsored content and engaging with other users to build a following.
7. **Comment bots:** Post comments on social media platforms, often in response to specific keywords or topics.
8. **Analytics bots:** Collect data on social media activity, such as likes, shares and comments.

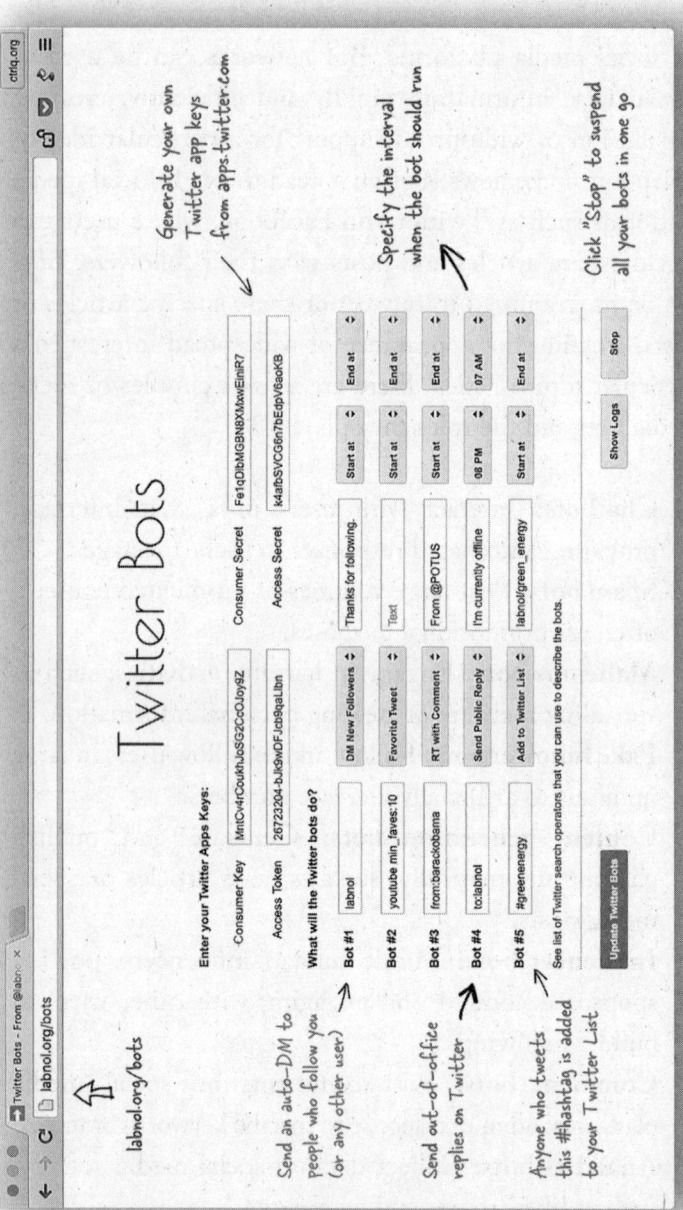

Source: Amit Agarwal's (2017) fairly accessible guide, How to Write a Twitter Bot in 5 Minutes.

Bot networks can also be used to amplify the reach of fake news by artificially inflating the number of likes, shares and comments on a post. This can make the post appear more popular and legitimate than it actually is, increasing its visibility and impact. To combat the spread of fake news, social media platforms have implemented various measures to identify and remove bots and fake accounts. However, bot creators are constantly developing new techniques to evade detection, making it an ongoing challenge for platforms to stay ahead of the game.

Social media bots can be used for a variety of purposes, ranging from harmless automated posting to more malicious activities such as spreading disinformation or manipulating public opinion. Some common attack methods of social media bots include:

1. **Spamming:** Flooding social media platforms with spam messages, links or advertisements, often in an attempt to lure users into clicking on malicious links.
2. **Fake news and disinformation:** Spreading false information and propaganda to influence public opinion on certain topics. This can be particularly effective during election campaigns, where bots can be used to sway voters.
3. **Impersonation:** Impersonating real people or organizations on social media platforms. This can be used to spread false information, promote propaganda or even conduct scams.
4. **Amplification:** Amplifying the reach of certain messages or content on social media platforms including

hate speech. This can be used to create a false sense of popularity or to spread propaganda more widely.

5. **Botnets:** Networks of bots that can be used for more advanced attacks, such as distributed denial-of-service (DDoS) attacks, which can overload a website or server with traffic, making it inaccessible.

6. **Account takeover:** Taking over legitimate social media accounts, either through phishing or other hacking methods. Once the account is compromised, the bot can use it to spread spam or malicious content.

7. **Click fraud:** Clicking on ads or other links in order to generate revenue for the bot operator. This can lead to inflated advertising costs for legitimate businesses and advertisers.

8. **Brute force attacks:** Bots can be used to attempt to guess passwords or other login credentials in order to gain access to social media accounts. This can be used to steal personal information or to spread spam or other malicious content.

There are various ways in which social media bots can be used, some of which include:

1. **Customer service:** Responding to customer queries and complaints on social media platforms, providing a quick and efficient way to address customer needs.

2. **Content sharing:** Sharing content on various social media platforms, such as blog posts, news articles and product updates.

3. **Lead generation:** Generating leads by interacting with users and collecting contact information from potential customers.

4. **Personalization:** Personalizing content for users by analysing interests and preferences and providing recommendations based on that information.

5. **Social listening:** Monitoring social media conversations and providing insights into trends and user sentiment.

6. **Influencer marketing:** Identifying and engaging with influencers, increasing brand awareness and driving sales.

7. **Polling and surveys:** Conducting polls and surveys to collect feedback from users on various topics.

8. **Automated posting:** Automating posting on social media platforms, such as scheduling posts at specific times and days.

"NICE ONE!" "AMAZING PHOTO"
"GOOD JOB!"
"COOL PIC"
"COOL!"
"NICE FEED"
"NICE PIC!"
"PERFECT ONE!"
"GREAT CONTENT"
*Some random emoji
that has nothing   "I LIKE YOUR PAGE"
to do with anything*
"THIS AM GOOD"   "VERY NICE! 😄"
                   *Some comment that
YADA YADA YADA.   has nothing to do
                   with the pic/video*

Source: ezanga.com—Instagram Bots designed to boost user social media presence[9]

It's important to be vigilant and critical when consuming news and information online. Always fact-check before sharing any articles or posts, and be wary of accounts that appear to be bots or automated. By staying informed and exercising caution, we can help reduce the spread of fake news and ensure that accurate information prevails.

Are bots winning the war? There are more bots on Twitter than you may think. There are so many fake accounts on Twitter that even Elon Musk initially shied away from the $44 billion takeover of Twitter. As of 2021, it was estimated that around 5 per cent to 32 per cent of all Twitter accounts were bots (Twitter claimed only 5 per cent).[10] On Instagram, it was estimated that around 9.5 per cent of all accounts were bots, and on Facebook, the number was estimated to be around 5 per cent. These are just estimates, and the actual number of bots on social media platforms may be higher or lower than these figures, depending on various factors such as the definition of bot and the methods used to detect them. It's also worth noting that not all bots are the same—some are harmless, while others can be used for malicious purposes such as spreading misinformation or manipulating public opinion. Social media bots are automated programs designed to perform tasks on social media platforms such as liking, commenting and following users. Here are some common signature behaviours of social media bots:

1. **High activity levels:** Social media bots are programmed to perform actions on a large scale and with high

frequency. This means they are likely to have higher activity levels than human users.

2. **Repetitive behaviours:** Social media bots often perform the same actions repeatedly, such as liking or retweeting content, or following and unfollowing users.

3. **Impersonal responses:** Bots tend to provide generic or pre-written responses to user interactions, rather than engaging in personalized conversations.

4. **Rapid response times:** Social media bots are designed to respond quickly to user interactions, often within seconds or minutes of receiving a message or comment.

5. **Low engagement levels:** While bots may generate high levels of activity, they tend to have lower engagement levels than human users. This is because they are not capable of generating the same level of personal connection as human interactions.

6. **Limited language capabilities:** Bots are typically programmed to understand and respond in a limited range of languages and dialects, and may not be able to understand certain slang or regional language variations.

7. **Zero or minimal user history:** Social media bots usually have no or minimal history of personal user interactions and are often created to perform specific tasks or promote certain content or products.

It is important to note that not all automated programs on social media are bots. Some programs, such as chatbots, are designed to provide personalized and interactive responses to user interactions. It is important to carefully evaluate the behaviour of any program or account on social media to determine whether it is a bot or a legitimate user.

Microtargeting and the Propagation of Fake News[11]

Cambridge Analytica was a data analytics firm that used microtargeting techniques to influence voters during political campaigns. Microtargeting is the practice of using data analysis and profiling techniques to identify specific groups of individuals who are likely to respond to particular messages or advertising. Cambridge Analytica obtained data on millions of Facebook users without their consent through a third-party app called 'This is your digital life'. This data was then used to create detailed profiles of individuals, including their interests, personalities and political leanings.[12] These profiles were then used to microtarget individuals with political advertising and messaging that was specifically tailored to appeal to their particular interests and beliefs. By using this approach, Cambridge Analytica claimed to be able to influence people's voting behaviour and opinions. There is evidence that Cambridge Analytica used microtargeting in several high-profile political campaigns, including the 2016 US presidential election and the Brexit referendum in the UK. However, the exact extent of their influence is still a matter of debate and investigation.

Microtargeting is a marketing technique that uses data analysis to identify specific groups of people and then deliver tailored messages to those groups. It has become increasingly popular in political campaigns, where it is used to identify and target potential supporters or swing voters with customized messages. While microtargeting can be a useful tool for reaching specific audiences with relevant information, it can also be used to propagate fake news. By using data analysis to identify people who are likely to be receptive to particular messages, unscrupulous actors can target those individuals with false or misleading information designed to influence their opinions and behaviour. Here are some examples of microtargeting:

1. **Political Campaigns:** Political campaigns use microtargeting to identify and target specific voters based on demographics, voting history and other data. For example, a campaign might use data to target a specific group of people who are likely to support their candidate or issue.

2. **Social Media Advertising:** Social media platforms like Facebook and Instagram use microtargeting to deliver ads to specific groups of people based on their interests, behaviour and other data. For example, an advertiser might target people who have shown an interest in a particular product or service.

3. **Email Marketing:** Email marketers use microtargeting to send personalized messages to specific groups of people based on their interests, behaviour and other data. For example, an e-commerce company might send a targeted email to customers who have previously purchased products in a particular category.

4. **Mobile App Advertising:** Mobile app developers use microtargeting to show ads to specific users based on their behaviour within the app. For example, a gaming app might show ads for other games to users who have previously shown an interest in gaming.

5. **Location-Based Advertising:** Location-based advertising uses microtargeting to deliver ads to people based on their physical location. For example, a coffee shop might use location-based advertising to target people who are within a certain distance of their shop.

How Is Fake News Directed at Specific Types of People?

The use of social media analytics is a common digital marketing strategy. Whenever a user visits a website, it prompts them to accept or reject the website's cookie policy. A cookie is a small text file that a website or an online service stores on a user's device. When the user visits the website or uses the service, cookies are used to remember the user's preferences and settings to authenticate the user, track the user's behaviour and provide personalized content and advertising. There are different types of cookies, including session cookies and persistent cookies. Session cookies are deleted when the user closes the browser, while persistent cookies remain on the user's device for a longer period of time unless the user deletes them or they expire. Cookies are often used by websites and online services to improve the user experience and to analyse the user's online behaviour. However, some users may be concerned about their privacy and security, as cookies can be used to track their activities and collect personal information. Therefore, many browsers and online services allow users to control and manage cookies, including blocking or deleting them. But all may not be well as websites may use cookie trackers to not only analyse your behaviour on their websites but also on other websites the user may visit. This may help them track your preferences and make them target the user with advertising and re-marketing campaigns. The website may also sell this information to third parties which may also target the user with all kinds of content, invading their privacy and manipulating or influencing their preferences.

Trolls and the Propagation of Fake News

Trolls and the propagation of fake news are interconnected phenomena that have become increasingly prevalent with the rise of social media. Trolls are individuals who deliberately seek to disrupt online discussions and provoke others through inflammatory or off-topic messages. They argue, insult and name-call even public figures. The troll's purpose is to dilute ideologies they do not follow and to intimidate those who do. They often use anonymity to avoid accountability for their actions. One of the ways trolls achieve their disruptive goals is by spreading fake news or misinformation. By sharing false information, they can stir up controversy, sow doubt and divide people into opposing camps. This can be especially effective in a polarized political climate, where people are already primed to accept information that confirms their biases and reject anything that challenges them.

Al Qaeda and ISIS have been known to use YouTube to post violent videos and exploit social media to build their network and orchestrate terrorist attacks in various countries. However, the impact of Russian trolls on American democracy during the 2016 US presidential election is unprecedented. There were allegations that Russian trolls, or individuals paid by the Russian government, engaged in spreading propaganda and disinformation on social media to influence the election result.

The Russian troll operation was reportedly carried out by the Internet Research Agency (IRA), a St Petersburg-based organization that has been linked to the Russian government.[13] According to various reports, the operation involved the creation of numerous fake social media accounts, which were used to spread false information and propaganda aimed at creating discord and confusion among the American electorate. The operation allegedly targeted key swing states and focused on promoting Donald Trump while denigrating his opponent, Hillary Clinton.

The extent to which the Russian troll operation influenced the outcome of the election remains a subject of debate, and the full extent of the operation's activities is not yet known. However, it is widely believed that the Russian troll operation had some impact on the election, particularly in terms of amplifying existing divisions and grievances within the American electorate. The primary goal of the Russian trolls was to sow discord and chaos in the American political system. They did this by spreading false information about candidates and issues, amplifying existing divisions in American society and generally creating an atmosphere of confusion and mistrust. One of the most notable ways in which the Russian trolls impacted the 2016 elections was through their use of social media platforms such as Facebook, Twitter and Instagram. They created and shared thousands of posts and messages that were designed to appeal to specific groups of voters, particularly those who were more susceptible to conspiracy theories and fake news. Besides this, the Russian trolls engaged in a variety of other tactics, such as creating fake news sites, running targeted ads and hacking into the email accounts of prominent political figures.

Russia's Social Media Influence Operations – Multi-platform, Full Spectrum		
Objective	Platforms	Purpose & Advantages
Placement	Primary: *4Chan, Reddit* Secondary: *8Chan, YouTube, Facebook*	• Insert forgeries into social media discussions • Seed conspiracies into target audiences • Spread kompromat on targeted adversaries, both true & false information • Hides Kremlin attribution, provides plausible deniability
Propagation	*Twitter*	• Spread narratives through overt Kremlin accounts & covert troll farm personas • Amplify select target audience stories & preferable narratives supporting Kremlin goals (*Computational propaganda make falsehoods appear more believable through repetition & volume*) • Inject stories into mainstream media worldwide • Attack political opponents, foreign policy experts & adversarial media personalities
Saturation	Primary: *Facebook* Secondary: *Google, LinkedIn, Instagram, Pinterest*	• Amplify political & social divisions, erode faith in democracy through discussions & ads • Pull content from other platforms into trusted friends & family discussions • Recruit target audience for organic propaganda creation/distribution or physical provocations (protests, rallies or even violence)
Hosting	*YouTube*	• Overt propaganda posts obscuring Kremlin hand (RT) • Sharing of video content to target audience via producers & reporters rather than standard television channels

Source: C. Watts (Foreign Policy Research Institute, Alliance For Securing Democracy, Center For Cyber & Homeland Security)

While some aspects of the Russian troll campaign have been uncovered by US social media platforms, the full extent of this operation remains unverified. The Russian social media campaign targeted American democracy in various stages, such as reconnaissance, hosting, placement, propagation and saturation. These social media accounts took American names and added connections, friends and followers to blend in as part of the American community.

Moving forward, addressing the future of fake news amplification is a complex and constantly evolving challenge. With the advancement of technology, the spread of misinformation has become more prevalent and sophisticated. Social media platforms, in particular, have played a significant role in amplifying fake news, as they provide an easy and efficient way for information to reach a large audience. There are several potential paths that the future of fake news amplification could take. One possibility is that social media platforms will take a more proactive approach to addressing the problem. This could involve implementing more stringent content moderation policies, investing in technology to detect and remove fake news and collaborating with fact-checking organizations to provide users with accurate information.

Another possibility is that fake news amplification could become even more widespread, as bad actors continue to develop new and more effective tactics for spreading misinformation. For example, deepfake technology could be used to create videos or audio recordings that are indistinguishable from real footage, making it even harder to identify what is true and what is not.

In the end, the future of fake news amplification will depend on a range of factors, including technological advancements, regulatory frameworks and the actions of social media platforms and users alike. However, one thing is clear: addressing this issue will require a concerted effort on the part of all stakeholders, including governments, tech companies and individuals, to ensure that accurate information prevails over falsehoods.

VIII

Truth Behind Fake News—Role of Fact-Checkers

'The media, in general, has shied away from fact-checking to a large extent because of fears that we'd be called biased, and also because I think it's hard journalism. It's a lot easier to give the on-the-one-hand, on-the-other-hand kind of journalism and leave it to readers to sort it out. But that isn't good enough these days. The information age has made things so chaotic, I think it's our obligation in the mainstream media to help people sort out what's true and what's not.'

—Bill Adair, founder of PolitiFact, in an interview with the *New York Times* (2010).

During the COVID-19 pandemic, the following recipe claiming that garlic is a cure for coronavirus did the rounds on social media: 'Good news, Wuhan's coronavirus can be cured by one bowl of freshly boiled garlic water. An old Chinese doctor has proven it's efficacy. Many patients have also proven this to be effective. Eight (8) cloves of chopped cloves of garlic add seven (7) cups of water and bring to a boil. Eat and drink the boiled garlic water, overnight improvement and healing. Glad to share this (sic).' This claim is false and unsupported by scientific evidence. The World Health Organization (WHO) has explicitly stated that there is no scientific evidence to suggest that eating garlic can protect people from the coronavirus.[1] While garlic does have some antimicrobial properties and may have some health benefits, it is not a cure for the virus.

The best way to protect yourself from COVID-19 is to follow guidelines issued by public health officials, such as washing your hands frequently, wearing masks and practising social distancing. If you think you may have been exposed to the virus or have symptoms, it is important to get tested and follow the advice of healthcare professionals.

There are a lot of myths in the form of fake news circulating on social media, which WHO has tried to address on its website. The WHO clarified that it is better to clean your hands frequently instead of wearing gloves, and that alcohol-based sanitizers can be used in regions where alcohol is prohibited. Taking vitamin and mineral supplements does not safeguard from the virus, neither does drinking alcohol or adding pepper to your diet, the WHO said. Cold weather and snow cannot kill the virus, the WHO added.

Number of COVID-19 deaths worldwide as of 2 May 2023 (Top five countries)

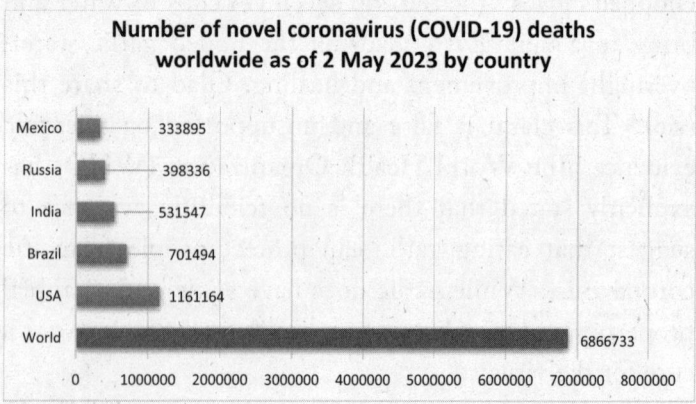

Source: Statista 2023[2]

Remember the 1984 supernatural comedy film *Ghostbusters* and the theme song,

> If there's somethin' strange in the neighbourhood
> Who ya gonna call (ghostbusters)
>
> There's somethin' weird and it don't look good
> Who ya gonna call (ghostbusters)

Fake news is a pervasive issue that confronts us daily. It lurks in our social media feeds and catches us on the wrong foot, taking advantage of our inability to distinguish between what is real and what is fake. In such circumstances, where you cannot distinguish between fake and real news, whom do you call? Fact-checker. A fact-checker is a person or organization that verifies the accuracy and truthiness of information presented in various forms of media, such as news articles, videos and social media posts. Fact-checkers investigate claims and statements to ensure that they are supported by evidence and are not misleading or false. Fact-checking is an important process in ensuring that the public has access to accurate and reliable information, particularly in the era of fake news and misinformation. Fact-checkers often work for news organizations, non-profits or independent fact-checking websites and are responsible for researching and verifying claims made by politicians, public figures and media outlets. They use various tools and techniques to investigate claims, including analysing data, conducting interviews and reviewing public records.

The role of fact-checkers is important for several reasons. First, they help to identify and correct false or misleading information that is being circulated. By doing so, they help to prevent the spread of harmful misinformation and reduce the impact of fake news.

Second, fact-checkers help to promote transparency and accountability in the media. By fact-checking claims and reporting on their findings, they help to hold individuals and organizations accountable for the accuracy of their statements.

Finally, fact-checkers help to promote critical thinking and media literacy. By providing accurate and trustworthy information, they help to equip individuals with the tools they need to make informed decisions and to distinguish between real news and fake news. The role of fact-checkers is essential in combating the spread of fake news. They play an important role in promoting transparency, accountability and critical thinking, and their work helps to ensure that individuals have access to accurate and trustworthy information.

There are several reputable fact-checking websites that specialize in verifying the accuracy of news stories and debunking fake news. Some of the most well-known ones include:

1. **FactCheck.org:** A nonpartisan, non-profit website that fact-checks political claims and statements made by politicians and public figures.
2. **Snopes.com:** A website that has been debunking urban legends, myths and misinformation since 1994.
3. **PolitiFact.com:** A fact-checking website that focuses on statements made by politicians and other public figures in the US.
4. **AP Fact Check:** A service provided by the Associated Press that checks the accuracy of news stories and viral social media posts.
5. **Reuters Fact Check:** A fact-checking service provided by the Reuters news agency that investigates claims made in the news and social media.
6. **Lead Stories:** A website that specializes in debunking hoaxes, fake news stories and conspiracy theories.
7. **Alt News:** It is a fact-checking website that focuses on verifying misinformation and fake news in India.

8. **Boom Live:** This website focuses on fact-checking political and social news in India.
9. **FactChecker.in:** This website provides independent, unbiased and factual analysis of news and public policy.
10. **Vishvas News:** It is a fact-checking website in Hindi that verifies and debunks fake news and misinformation.
11. **The Quint:** It is an online news portal that has a dedicated section for fact-checking and debunking misinformation.
12. **Newschecker.in:** It is a fact-checking website that verifies news and information across a wide range of topics, including politics, health and technology.
13. **India Today Fact Check:** This website is part of the India Today Group and focuses on fact-checking claims and statements made by politicians and public figures.
14. **AFP Fact Check India:** It is a fact-checking website run by Agence France-Presse (AFP), which verifies the accuracy of news stories and social media posts.

It is always a good idea to fact-check news stories before sharing them on social media or believing them to be true. These websites can be a helpful resource in verifying the accuracy of information circulating on the internet.

The Methodology

Fact-checking is the process of verifying the accuracy and credibility of information presented as factual. Fact-checking requires a rigorous and systematic approach to evaluating information and ensuring that the public has access to accurate and reliable information. Fake news fact-checking sites typically work by using a combination of automated algorithms and human editors to evaluate the accuracy of news stories and other types of content. First, the content is analysed using natural language processing algorithms and other machine learning techniques to identify potentially false or misleading information. This may involve checking the content against existing databases of verified facts, examining the credibility of the sources cited and looking for patterns of bias or distortion. Once the automated analysis is complete, human editors review the content to make a final determination about its accuracy. This may involve conducting additional research, contacting relevant experts or eyewitnesses and evaluating the overall context and tone of the content. Finally, the results of the fact-checking process are published on the website in the form of a rating or a detailed explanation of the reasons why the content is considered false or misleading. Some fact-checking sites also provide additional resources to help readers understand how to identify and evaluate fake news on their own.

The methodology for fact-checking typically involves the following steps:

1. **Selection of the Claim:** The first step in fact-checking is to select a claim that needs to be checked. This could

be a statement made by a public figure, a news article or a social media post.

2. **Research:** The next step is to gather as much information as possible about the claim. This may involve reading the original source, researching the topic online and consulting relevant experts or organizations.

3. **Verification:** Once the information is gathered, the fact-checker needs to verify the accuracy of the claim. This may involve fact-checking the sources cited, checking for biases or conflicts of interest and checking for any errors or omissions in the information.

4. **Analysis:** After verifying the accuracy of the claim, the fact-checker needs to analyse the information and determine whether the claim is true, false or somewhere in between. This may involve weighing the evidence and evaluating the credibility of the sources.

5. **Conclusion:** Finally, the fact-checker needs to draw a conclusion about the claim and present their findings in a clear and concise manner. This may involve providing additional context or explaining why the claim is true or false.

Snopes.com's 'Transparency' page talks about its methodology for fact-checking fake news.[3] Their methodology involves a thorough investigation of the claims made in a particular story or post. They rely on a combination of various sources, including interviews with experts, government agencies, news reports and historical archives. They also use fact-checking tools to verify the accuracy of the information presented in the claims. Snopes.com applies a rigorous process that includes the following steps:

1. **Initial research and examination:** They gather as much information as possible about the claim, including the source and the context in which it was made. They contact the source for elaboration and supporting information and individuals or organizations who are subject or area experts. They also consult secondary sources which may be related to the topic. Their editors analyse the claim and identify any potential issues or discrepancies. This includes checking the credibility of the sources and verifying the accuracy of the information presented.

2. **Topic selection:** Snopes.com focuses not just on political fact-checking but also on other topics which need not necessarily be important, controversial or superficial. Their paramount focus is on readers' interest which they find out through their social listening tools, emails received from readers, keyword analysis on search engines, etc. They are selective in their approach, and the selection of topics is done at their discretion.

3. **Source:** Snopes uses non-partisan information and scientific data sources like government-issued reports and peer-reviewed journals. Each fact-checked article will have an expandable 'source' tab at the foot of the article. This will give references used to fact-check the article.

    For example, the latest article listed on snopes.com on 1 April 2023 is, 'Will Trump Be Handcuffed During

His Arraignment on Hush-Money Charges?' by Alex Kasprak, an investigative journalist with snopes.com.

The Claim: 'As part of his arraignment on charges stemming from a grand jury indictment in New York, former president Donald Trump will be handcuffed.'

Snopes Rating: Unproven

Context: 'In sum, experts with knowledge of the Manhattan DA's office, Secret Service, and NYPD have all expressed doubt that Trump will be handcuffed or publicly displayed as part of his arraignment, and Trump's legal team has said that an agreement has been reached that he will not be cuffed. However, such an agreement would go against typical practices and the ultimate authority on these questions lies with Bragg (Alvin Bragg, Manhattan DA). As such, the claim is unproven.'

Reference Source: William K. Rashbaum, 'This Is What Will Happen When Trump Is Arrested in the Coming Days', *New York Times*, 30 March 2023, https://www.nytimes.com/2023/03/30/nyregion/indictment-meaning-trump-arrest.html.

Snopes.com also includes detailed explanations of their findings and sources, allowing users to verify the information for themselves.

Facts that are checked on snopes.com are rated so that people can understand the credibility of that claim quickly. Some of these ratings are:

- Research In Progress
- True
- Mostly True
- False
- Mostly False
- Unfound
- Unproven
- Scam

Overall, Snopes.com's methodology is based on thorough research and verification, ensuring that the information presented is accurate and reliable. India, like many other countries, has experienced an increase in the spread of fake news in recent years. Some of the most common types of fake news in India include political propaganda, misinformation related to health and science, and hoaxes related to social issues.

In 2018, the Indian government announced a new initiative called the 'Fact-Check Unit' to combat fake news. The unit is part of the Press Information Bureau (PIB) and is responsible for identifying and debunking fake news stories that are circulated in the Indian media.

Additionally, there are several fact-checking websites and organizations in India that work to identify and debunk fake news. Some of the prominent ones include

Alt-News, BOOM Live, and FactChecker.in. These organizations use various methods such as verification of sources, fact-checking tools and expert opinions to verify the accuracy of news stories. However, despite the efforts of the government and independent organizations, the spread of fake news in India continues to be a significant problem. Social media platforms, such as WhatsApp and Facebook, are often used to spread fake news rapidly, and it can be challenging to track down the source of these stories.

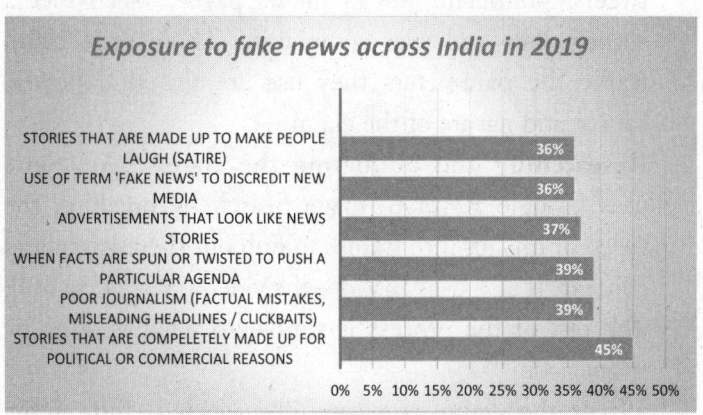

Source: Statista 2023 Exposure to fake news across India in 2019[4]

Another example from India is altnews.in. Altnews.in is a fact-checking website that aims to counter misinformation and fake news circulating on social media and other online platforms. Altnews.in verifies and debunks claims made in news articles, social media posts and other online sources by providing evidence-based articles and reports. The website covers a wide range of topics including politics, society, health and science. It also provides tools and resources for individuals and organizations to combat misinformation and promote fact-based journalism. Altnews.in has gained a reputation for its accuracy, credibility and transparency, and is widely respected as a reliable source of information in India. The methodology for fact-checking which Alt News follows is:[5]

1. **Selecting a claim to be debunked:** They track speeches, tweets, politicians' social media pages, social media suspect lists and user complaints. To manage claim traffic the parameters they use are the viral power, source and nature of the claim.
2. **Researching and evaluating the claims:** Alt-News uses Google Reverse Image Search by breaking the video or images into frames to find out their origin and context. It also uses InVid—the video verification tool. The rest of the process is similar to what is done by snopes.com
3. When the claims are carefully selected, thoroughly researched and scientifically evaluated, they are put in the public domain in the form of easy-to-understand articles and are updated from time to time.

Fact-Checking the 'Fact-Checker'

With the growing importance of fact-checking, it is important to critically examine the methodology and practices of fact-checkers.

In many cases, the tools used to check facts may be inadequate for the statement or claim in question. For example, in politics, the subject matter is itself so complex that multiple interpretations can arise even with scientific evaluation, making it difficult to determine the credibility of fact-checkers. Even when a statement is proved to be wrong, the politician who made that statement cannot be termed a liar. It is natural that in such circumstances people may naturally disagree with the truth. This is why we see politicians making statements like, 'Mahatma Gandhi didn't have a university degree.'[6]

Political statements often involve exaggerations, misrepresentations, selective truths and distortion of facts. Therefore, it becomes a challenge for fact-checkers to classify these statements as true or false.

With political figures making numerous supposedly factual statements during elections, it becomes an impossible task for fact-checkers to verify them all. Notably, Bill Adair, the founder of PolitiFact, said in an interview that Donald Trump is an outlier, with over half of his statements rated as false, more than any other presidential candidate.

This raises questions about the relevance of fact-checking and whether people prioritize truth or lies when voting for their preferred candidate. Fact-checkers play an important role in selecting which statements or claims to evaluate. Similar to case selection in social science research, it is crucial to test and prove a hypothesis without biased or predetermined outcomes.

If the fact-checker's selection of statements, for example, between Narendra Modi and Rahul Gandhi, is not scientific, it may lead to a perception of dishonesty based on the number of false statements.

Does this mean the sampling methods employed by fact-checkers are flawed? Let us consider an example. Suppose Narendra Modi and Rahul Gandhi make 100 statements each ahead of an upcoming election. Rahul Gandhi makes five false statements, while Modi makes fifty false statements. The fact-checker chooses a sample of five statements from each candidate, deeming them to be lies. Consequently, the fact-checker declares that 100 per cent of the sample statements are false. However, Rahul Gandhi has a 95 per cent accuracy rate, while Modi has a 50 per cent accuracy rate. However, the sampling procedure chosen by the fact-checker makes both Modi and Gandhi look dishonest in their electoral campaign speeches or statements. This shows that not using a scientific sampling method and cherry-picking statements can result in an inaccurate portrayal of the person.

Moreover, it is true that many fact-checkers are political journalists who, despite their best intentions, may be biased towards a particular political ideology. This cognitive bias can hinder their ability to select an unbiased sample of statements or claims. While most fact-checkers claim to choose statements in the interest of the public, it remains a matter of debate as it is difficult to accurately determine the public's interest. Conducting scientifically researched surveys consistently every week or month may be impractical. Consequently, the selection process may rely on the fact-checker's gut feeling. In such cases, the best approach is to identify all political statements and then randomly sample them to ensure fairness and accuracy.

Claims by Data and Statistics

Fact-checking political claims can be a challenging task, especially when it comes to data and statistics. Fact-checking data and statistics in political claims is an essential part of ensuring the accuracy and truthiness of information presented to the public. Data and statistics can have a significant impact on political claims. Political claims are often made in an attempt to persuade people to adopt a certain point of view or to support a particular policy or candidate. When data and statistics are used effectively, they can help to make a political claim more compelling and persuasive.

One way that data and statistics can be used in political claims is to provide evidence to support an argument. For example, a politician might claim that their policies have led to a decrease in unemployment rates. To support this claim, they might provide statistics that show a decrease in unemployment over the time period in which their policies were implemented. This type of evidence can help convince people that the politician's policies are effective. Another way that data and statistics can be used in political claims is to frame an issue in a particular way. Politicians might use statistics to highlight the severity of a problem, such as poverty or crime rates, in order to gain support for their policies aimed at addressing the problem. On the other hand, they might use statistics to downplay the significance of a problem if they do not have a solution to offer. However, the use of data and statistics in political claims can also be misleading. Statistics can be manipulated or selectively chosen to support a particular argument or to make a situation appear better or worse than it really is. It is important for individuals to critically evaluate the data and statistics presented in political claims and to consider the source and potential biases before making a decision.

Factchecker.in, India's fact-checking site, found out that there were 43 claims made by Prime Minister Narendra Modi between 2014 and 2019 that were untrue. Some of them are as follows:[7]

Claim

← **Tweet**

 PMO India ✔   ...
@PMOIndia
⚑ India government organization

सोचिए, आखिर क्यों, आजादी के बाद के 67 वर्षों तक केवल 70 प्रतिशत ग्रामीण परिवारों तक ही बिजली की सुविधा पहुंची थी और अब कैसे बीते चार वर्षों में 95 प्रतिशत ग्रामीण परिवारों तक बिजली पहुंच गई है: PM @narendramodi
Translate Tweet

11:19 AM · Dec 7, 2018

316 Retweets   **13** Quotes   **1,320** Likes   **3** Bookmarks

Source: FactChecker

(Why is it that even after 67 years of independence, only 70 per cent of the rural households were electrified, while in the last four years alone, 95 per cent of the rural households have been electrified)

Fact-check: False. By the time BJP came to power in 2014, 97 per cent of villages were already electrified, and only 3 per cent (18,452) were left to be connected to the grid. By 2018, BJP declared 100 per cent electrification of the rural villages, but in reality, of these 3 per cent unelectrified villages, only 8 per cent were connected to the grid.[8]

The date was 21 January 2017, and the occasion was the swearing-in ceremony of Donald Trump as America's 45th president. Then, White House press secretary Sean Spicer made a false statement that the crowd gathered to witness Trump's swearing-in was the largest in the history of presidential swearing-in ceremonies. Snopes.com debunked this claim as false. While the National Park Service stopped providing official crowd estimates in the 1990s, visual evidence and data from transportation and security agencies indicate that the crowd at President Trump's swearing-in was significantly smaller than the crowd at President Obama's 2009 inauguration. Additionally, photos of the National Mall taken at both events clearly show that Obama's inauguration had a larger crowd.[9] Therefore, it was inaccurate to claim that Trump's inauguration crowd was the largest in history.

In another case, Amit Malviya, national IT cell head of the Bharatiya Janata Party (BJP), claimed that the Shaheen Bagh protests were sponsored. The Shaheen Bagh protests began in December 2019 as a response to the Citizenship Amendment Act (CAA), which was passed by the Indian government. The protests took place in Shaheen Bagh, a Muslim-majority neighbourhood in Delhi, and were led by women who sat in a peaceful sit-in protest for several months. Various individuals and groups made different claims regarding the funding of the Shaheen Bagh protests. Malviya tweeted a video claiming that the women protesters were paid INR 500–700 per day. However, it is worth noting that the claim has not been substantiated. The organizers of the Shaheen Bagh protests have maintained that the protests were entirely peaceful and spontaneous, and they were not funded or sponsored by any organization. It is essential to note that in a democratic society, citizens have the right to protest and express their dissent without any fear of reprisal or accusations of wrongdoing, as long as it is done in a peaceful manner and within the boundaries of the law.

English news channel Times Now broadcast the video posted by Amit Malviya from his Twitter handle. Times Now's Megha Prasad was sceptical about the source of the video and questioned the 'sting operation' conducted to record the video. Both India Today TV and Republic TV debated this in their primetime debates and Republic TV even went ahead and ran a #Protestonhire hashtag on Twitter, insinuating that the Congress party was behind the protest.[10]

Alt-News watched the video frame by frame and found a mobile number in the video, which they tracked down to a telecom retail outlet in the area of Tughlakabad, New Delhi, a shop owned by Ashwani Kumar, who is suspected to have shot the video that became viral.

The Epistemological Critique of Fact-Checking

Objective practice and fact-checking are both crucial components of producing accurate information and maintaining the integrity of the knowledge production process. Objective practice refers to the systematic and unbiased approach to gathering and analysing information, whereas fact-checking involves verifying the accuracy of information and claims made by individuals or organizations. However, the epistemology of fact-checking can be contested, particularly in the context of subjective or politically charged issues. Some argue that fact-checking is inherently biased, as the selection of claims to fact-check, the criteria for determining what constitutes a fact and the interpretation of evidence are all subject to interpretation.

Additionally, the fact-checking process can be influenced by the political leanings or biases of the fact-checkers themselves, potentially leading to selective fact-checking or a failure to fact-check claims that align with their personal beliefs. This has led to criticism from some quarters that fact-checking can perpetuate a biased perspective and contribute to a lack of trust in the media and other knowledge-producing institutions. Despite these criticisms, objective practice and fact-checking remain essential tools for ensuring the accuracy and integrity of the knowledge production process. However, it is important to acknowledge the potential for biases and contested interpretations in the fact-checking process and to work towards minimizing these effects through transparent and objective methods.

The epistemological critique of fact-checking is the idea that fact-checking, while well-intentioned, is inherently flawed and cannot be relied upon to determine the truthiness of a claim. The critique argues that the traditional fact-checking process is based on a flawed epistemological assumption that objective truth can be established through verification and that there is a clear distinction between facts and opinions. According to this critique, the fact-checking process assumes that there is a neutral and objective reality that can be observed and verified through empirical evidence. However, this assumption is problematic because our perceptions and interpretations of reality are influenced by our social, cultural and political context. This means that what one person considers to be a fact may be perceived differently by someone else. Furthermore, the critique argues that the distinction between facts and opinions is not always clear-cut. While some claims may be easily verifiable, others may be more complex and require interpretation and analysis. Additionally, the way in which facts are presented and contextualized can influence how they are perceived and understood.

Finally, the critique argues that fact-checking is often conducted by individuals or organizations with their own biases and interests, which can influence their assessment of the truthiness of a claim. Therefore, the fact-checking process cannot be fully objective and neutral. In summary, the epistemological critique of fact-checking argues that the fact-checking process is based on flawed assumptions about objective truth and the distinction between facts and opinions. It also highlights the influence of our social and cultural context, the complexity of some claims and the potential bias of fact-checkers themselves.

The Truth of Varying Shades

The language used by news media in the context of political fact-checking and fake news detection is crucial in ensuring accuracy and credibility. News outlets must use clear and objective language that avoids any biases or prejudices. One important aspect of language in political fact-checking and fake news detection is the use of verifiable sources. News outlets must use reliable sources and provide evidence to support their claims, rather than relying on unverified or uncorroborated information. Another important aspect is the use of precise and unambiguous language. News outlets must avoid using vague or overly general language that can be interpreted in different ways. Instead, they should use specific terms and provide clear definitions of key concepts and ideas. In addition, news outlets must avoid using emotional language that can be misleading or manipulative. Instead, they should focus on presenting the facts in a neutral and objective manner.

What Are the Linguistic Characteristics of a False Text?

A false text can exhibit a number of linguistic characteristics that differentiate it from a genuine text. False texts may contain errors or inconsistencies in grammar and syntax, which can make them sound unnatural or awkward. It may lack coherence or logical structure, making it difficult to follow the argument or message. It may use inappropriate or uncommon vocabulary, which can suggest that the text was written by someone with limited language skills or knowledge. False texts may display inconsistencies in tone and style, which can make them sound insincere or manipulative. It may contain false or misleading information, which can suggest that the text was written with a specific agenda or bias. Also, false texts may use excessive emotional language, which can be used to manipulate the reader's emotions rather than provide factual information. Finally, false texts may lack credibility due to the source or author, which can suggest that the text was written with a specific agenda or motive.

False texts may lack the clarity, coherence and credibility that is typically found in genuine texts, and may exhibit various linguistic features that make them stand out as being false or manipulated. Let us understand this example:

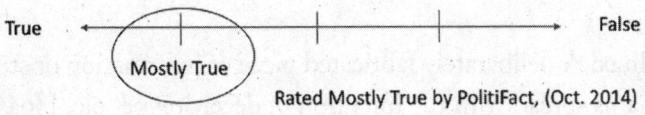

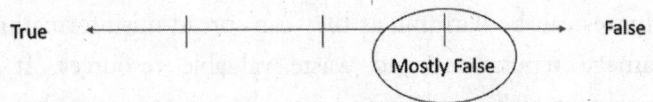

Source: 'Truth of Varying Shades: Analyzing Language in Fake News and Political Fact-Checking'[11]

The example above shows quotes rated by PolitiFact. As we see, there are components that contribute to the misleading nature of the statements. Without the word 'just', the first statement would be true, while the second statement is 'False' due to the correlation drawn between Google Search Trend and Brexit, which actually does not exist. The presence of 'misleading phrasing' in red, causes the ratings to fall between 'Mostly True' and 'Mostly False'. This characteristic of misleading phrasing leads many fact-checkers to assign in-between ratings, leaving the public uncertain about whether to consider them as 'True' or 'False'.

In order to analyse general news, fact-checkers categorize them into four types: trusted news, hoax, satire and propaganda. To understand the trustworthiness of these categories, let us first understand their true meanings.

Hoax: A deliberately fabricated piece of information or story that is spread with the intention of deceiving people. Hoaxes can take many forms, such as fake news stories, viral social media posts or even practical jokes. The purpose of a hoax can vary, but often it is to create confusion or panic, to make a political or social statement or to gain attention or fame. Hoaxes can be harmful, as they can spread misinformation, damage reputations and waste valuable resources. It is important to be vigilant and fact-check information before sharing it with others to prevent the spread of hoaxes.

Satire: A form of humour that uses irony, sarcasm and exaggeration to criticize or mock individuals, groups or society. Political satire often targets politicians, political issues and political institutions with the aim of exposing flaws or commenting on current events. It mimics real news but still cues the public to not take it seriously.

Propaganda: A form of communication that aims to influence the attitudes, beliefs and behaviours of people towards a particular idea, cause or group. It often involves the use of biased or misleading information to manipulate public opinion.

These news types can be categorized along two dimensions to understand the truthiness of the news in relation to the intent of the author.

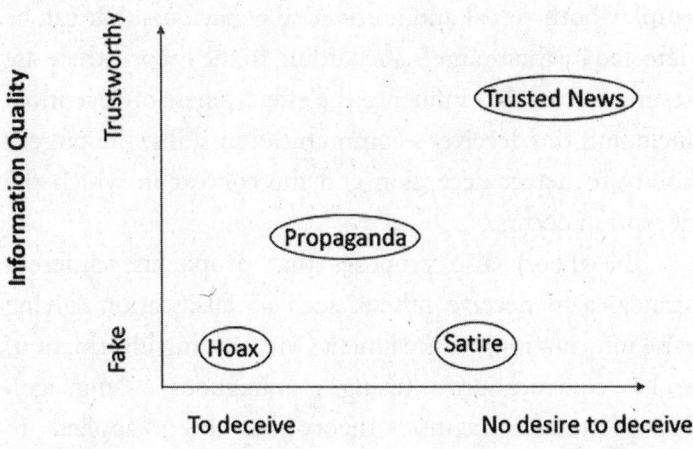

Source: 'Truth of Varying Shades: Analyzing Language in Fake News and Political Fact-Checking'[12]

The author's intention is a concern, especially when they represent people and are responsible for framing legislative laws in the country. If the intention of the author is to deceive the public through linguistic communication or misleading phrasing of statements, it becomes the responsibility of the fact-checker to uncover the truth by evaluating these statements and the level of deception. This type of communication is explained by the 'Interpersonal Deception Theory', which is a communication theory that seeks to explain how people deceive others in interpersonal interactions. Developed by David Buller and Judee Burgoon in the late 1990s, the theory recognizes that deception is a complex process involving both the deceiver and the target. It suggests that when people try to deceive others, they employ both verbal and non-verbal behaviours that can be detected by their targets. According to the theory, there are several factors that influence the effectiveness of deception, including the deceiver's communication skills, the target's ability to detect deception and the context in which the deception occurs.

The theory also proposes that people use different strategies to deceive others, such as falsification (giving false information), concealment (withholding information) and equivocation (using ambiguous language). Interpersonal deception theory has been applied to various contexts, including law enforcement, politics and romantic relationships. It has also been used to develop training programmes to help people detect deception. Psycholinguistic work in interpersonal deception theory postulated that in certain political statements or speech, the truth is deliberately not stated. Psycholinguistics is the study of the relationship between language and the mind. Interpersonal deception theory explains how people use deceptive language in interpersonal communication. Here are some examples of psycholinguistic work in interpersonal deception theory:

1. **Analysis of linguistic cues:** Psycholinguistic researchers have examined linguistic cues that are associated with deception, such as the use of fewer pronouns and more negative emotion words. These cues can be used to identify when someone is being deceptive.

2. **Analysis of cognitive processing:** Psycholinguistic researchers have also examined the cognitive processes involved in deceptive communication, such as the mental effort required to create a deceptive message and the cognitive load that accompanies lying.

3. **Analysis of non-verbal behaviour:** Psycholinguistic research has also examined non-verbal behaviour, such as facial expressions and body language, in relation to deception. This research has shown that non-verbal behaviour can also be used to detect deception.

4. **Analysis of deception in different contexts:** Psycholinguistic research has also explored deception in different contexts, such as online communication or in a second language. This research has shown that the cues associated with deception may vary depending on the context.

All said and done, the role of fact-checkers is vital in today's age of information overload. It is evolving as it is still in a nascent stage.

The future of fact-checking looks promising as the need for accurate information in the age of information overload continues to increase. Here are a few potential trends and developments in the world of fact-checking:

1. **Increased use of technology:** Fact-checking organizations are already using automated tools like AI and machine learning to help them sift through vast amounts of data and identify potentially misleading or

false information. As these technologies continue to improve, we can expect to see more widespread use of them in the fact-checking process.

2. **Collaboration between fact-checking organizations:** Fact-checking organizations often operate independently, but as the need for accurate information becomes more pressing, we may see more collaboration and sharing of resources between different fact-checking organizations.

3. **Focus on visual misinformation:** With the rise of deepfakes and other forms of visual misinformation, fact-checkers are beginning to develop new tools and strategies to combat these types of false information.

4. **Greater emphasis on education:** Many fact-checking organizations are starting to prioritize education and outreach, in addition to their fact-checking work. By teaching people how to spot false information and become more critical consumers of news, these organizations hope to prevent the spread of misinformation in the first place.

Overall, the future of fact-checking is likely to involve a combination of technological advancements, collaboration and education, all aimed at providing accurate information in an increasingly complex and fast-paced world.

IX

How to Protect and Defend Yourself from Fake News

'Fake sites, bots and trolls can falsify opinions. The fact is that today, certain algorithms can act as self-generating opinions *and we have to learn to deal with this.*'
—Angela Merkel, former chancellor of Germany

Many people might have fallen for fake news stories during their regular news consumption. Navigating through loads of targeted information can be challenging. Even the most intelligent and aware news consumers can find it difficult to distinguish between real and fake news. The overload of information through multiple sources and its amplification through social media makes news consumption for individuals an automatic and unconscious action. Information overload greatly contributes to the spread of fake news. When people are bombarded with an overwhelming amount of information, they may not have the time or inclination to fact-check every piece of information they come across. As a result, fake news and misinformation can spread rapidly, as people may be more likely to accept and share information without verifying its accuracy.

In an environment of information overload, people may also rely on shortcuts and heuristics to help them make sense of the information they are receiving. For example, they may be more likely to trust information that confirms their pre-existing beliefs or information that comes from a source they perceive to be trustworthy, without questioning its accuracy. This can make it easier for fake news to gain traction, as people may be more willing to believe and share information that reinforces their world view, even if it is false.

News consumption can become overwhelming and even automated in some cases. Many people may find themselves mindlessly scrolling through news feeds or consuming news content without much conscious thought. Fake news as a result of communication errors, editorial errors or poor internal decisions has a detrimental effect on a person's decision-making skills as it can undermine existing knowledge and beliefs. To win the fight against fake news, people should learn how to combat powerful disinformation campaigns. In this chapter, we examine how people can protect themselves from being deceived by fake news and regain a sense of control over news consumption.

Fake news can have a significant impact on people's lives, both individually and collectively as it spreads false information, which can lead people to make incorrect decisions based on inaccurate data. This can result in a range of negative consequences, from personal choices to public policies. Many such fake news stories have been circulated globally which have led to negative consequences for individuals, businesses and society at large. Fake news is becoming increasingly prevalent in today's society, particularly with the rise of social media and the ease of sharing information online. While it is difficult to determine the exact prevalence of fake news, studies have shown that it is a growing problem and can have significant negative impacts on individuals. The impact of fake news can vary depending on the individual and the nature of the misinformation. In some cases, fake news can lead to confusion or misunderstanding, while in other cases it can lead to fear, anger or even violence. For example, a false rumour about a terrorist attack or a public health crisis can cause panic and harm to individuals and communities. Also, fake news can undermine trust in institutions, including the media and government, and erode confidence in democratic processes. It can also contribute to the spread of conspiracy theories and other forms of misinformation that can harm individuals and society as a whole.

Why Are Individuals Attracted to Fake News?

To defend oneself from fake news, it is necessary to understand why we are drawn to it. One of the reasons why fake news can spread quickly on social media is because it often taps into the reader's emotions, biases and preconceptions of the reader, making it more appealing. Fake news stories can be designed to elicit strong emotional responses, such as anger, fear or excitement, which can lead to increased engagement and sharing. They can be tailored to align with pre-existing beliefs or opinions, making them more likely to be accepted and shared by individuals who are predisposed to believe them. This creates an echo chamber effect, where individuals are more likely to encounter and share information that confirms their existing beliefs while dismissing conflicting information.

Fake news stories often contain sensational or shocking elements that grab people's attention. These stories can be more engaging than mundane news, even if they lack factual basis. Moreover, social media algorithms are designed to prioritize content that generates high levels of engagement, which can contribute to the spread of fake news. When users engage with and share fake news stories, these algorithms may promote them to a wider audience, creating a self-reinforcing cycle of misinformation.

Is This Because Fake News Is Fascinating to the Brain?

The human brain is a complex organ responsible for receiving, processing and interpreting information from the environment. Fake news can be fascinating to the brain due to its ability to quickly capture attention, exploiting the brain's limited attention span. People tend to pay more attention to information that is surprising, emotionally arousing or aligning with their pre-existing beliefs. Another way to understand this is that humans are naturally drawn to novelty and the unexpected, and fake news often presents a twist on familiar topics. This can trigger a dopamine release in the brain, which is associated with pleasure and reward, and can make fake news feel inherently interesting and engaging. Also, fake news can tap into our emotions and beliefs, which can be powerful motivators. If a fake news story confirms something we already believe or supports our preconceived notions, we may be more likely to believe it and find it appealing. The way that fake news is often presented—with attention-grabbing headlines, sensationalistic language and dramatic imagery—can make it seem more important and urgent than other news stories. This can lead us to prioritize fake news over more accurate and reliable sources of information, which can have negative consequences for our understanding of the world around us.

It is an established fact that the brain relies on memory to store and retrieve information. Fake news can exploit the limitations of human memory, such as the misinformation effect, where people incorporate false information into their memories. The misinformation effect is a phenomenon where misleading information can alter a person's recollection of an event. This can happen when inconsistent information is incorporated into their memory, leading to distorted recollections of the event. The misinformation effect has been studied extensively in psychology and has important implications for eyewitness testimony and other forms of memory recall. For example, in criminal investigations, witnesses may be exposed to misleading information or suggestive questioning, which can lead to inaccurate recollections of events and potentially wrongful convictions.

There are several factors that can contribute to the misinformation effect, including the source of the misinformation, the timing and frequency of exposure to the misleading information and the individual's own cognitive processes and biases. To minimize the impact of the misinformation effect, it is important to use caution when presenting information that could potentially alter a person's memory, and to be aware of the potential for bias and suggestibility in eyewitness testimony and other forms of memory recall. The misinformation effect and fake news are related in that both involve the spread of false or misleading information. However, the misinformation effect typically occurs on a smaller scale, affecting individual memories of events, while fake news can have broader societal impacts. Both phenomena highlight the importance of critical thinking and fact-checking when evaluating information.

What Are the Main Motivations for Sharing Fake News on Social Media?

According to statista.com, as of January 2023, there were approximately 5.2 billion internet users worldwide, which is around 64.4 per cent of the global population.[1] Internet penetration rates vary widely by region, with the highest rates found in North America (91.8 per cent) and Europe (93.5 per cent), and the lowest rates in Africa (39.4 per cent) and Asia (52.4 per cent). Social media has also become increasingly popular in recent years. As of 2023, social media penetration is around 4.76 billion or 59.4 per cent of the worldwide population. The highest social media penetration rates are found in North America (77.8 per cent) and South America (66.7 per cent), while the lowest rates are found in Africa (12.6 per cent) and Central Asia (11.6 per cent). It's worth noting that these numbers are constantly changing as access to technology and the internet continues to expand around the world.[2]

Sharing misinformation can become habitual, rather than just a result of laziness or bias. Research has shown that individuals are more likely to share misinformation if they have previously shared it or if it aligns with their pre-existing beliefs.[3] One factor that contributes to the habitual sharing of misinformation is the way information spreads on social media platforms. Algorithms are designed to show users content that is most likely to engage them, which can lead to the amplification of misinformation that is attention-grabbing or emotionally charged. This creates an environment in which individuals are incentivized to share content that may not be accurate but is likely to generate engagement. Another factor is the cognitive bias known as confirmation bias, which is the tendency for individuals to seek out and believe information that confirms their pre-existing beliefs. This can lead to individuals sharing misinformation that reinforces their world view, even if it is not based on fact. Finally, misinformation can also be shared habitually as a result of social norms. If an individual's peers regularly share on social media platforms, they may develop a 'fear of missing out' (FOMO) and may feel pressured to do the same in order to fit in. In this race, speed matters and therefore the individual might end up sharing inaccurate information.

In many cases, sensationalism is the motive behind sharing fake news. Sensationalism is a form of media bias that focuses on shocking or attention-grabbing stories at the expense of accuracy or context. It can be considered a form of media bias, as it involves exaggerating or sensationalizing news stories in order to grab people's attention and generate higher ratings or more clicks. By focusing on the most dramatic or attention-grabbing aspects of a story, rather than providing a balanced and nuanced account, sensationalism can distort people's perceptions of events and issues, and create a distorted view of reality. Some examples of sensationalist reporting include using hyperbolic headlines or images that are unrelated to the story, relying on anonymous sources or rumours rather than verified information and focusing on emotional or shocking details rather than the broader context of a story. This can have real-world consequences, such as influencing public opinion or even policy decisions. While some degree of editorializing and interpretation is inevitable in news reporting, it is important for media outlets to strive for accuracy, balance and responsible journalism. By avoiding sensationalism and presenting information in a fair and objective manner, media organizations can help ensure that the public is well-informed and able to make informed decisions about the world around them.

Sensationalism can also play into people's emotions and biases, making them more likely to believe and share fake news that confirms their pre-existing opinions. For example, a sensationalized headline about a political scandal may appeal to someone who already distrusts a particular politician or a political party, leading them to share the story without fact-checking it. Therefore, sensationalism in media can be a powerful motivator for people to share fake news, as it plays into their emotions and biases and can make them more likely to believe and share misleading information. When people share fake news, they may be doing so in order to get attention or to generate clicks, likes or shares on social media. However, it's important to note that not all cases of fake news are driven by sensationalism. There are other factors that can lead to the creation and spread of fake news, such as political or ideological agendas, financial gain or simply a lack of understanding about what constitutes credible information. Additionally, people may share fake news unknowingly or without realizing that it is inaccurate. Regardless of the motive behind sharing fake news, it can have serious consequences, such as misinforming the public, damaging reputations and even inciting violence or social unrest. It's important for individuals to be critical consumers of information and to verify the accuracy of news stories before sharing them.

Social relationships and the user's social status or reputation are relevant indicators for news sharing. When people share news, they often do so with their friends, family and colleagues. The strength of the relationship between the sharer and the recipient can influence whether or not the news is shared. The user's social status or reputation can also play a role in news sharing. People with a higher social status or reputation may have more influence and credibility, and therefore their news-sharing behaviour may be more impactful. For example, a celebrity sharing a news article may have a greater reach and influence than an ordinary person. But it is risky too, as influencers can have their reputation and their social relationships damaged if they are found to be sharing fake news. Fake news formats are meant to not only deceive but also to go viral on social media.

Fake news can be used as a fraudulent strategy to make money from programmatic advertising on the web. This is because programmatic advertising platforms use algorithms to serve ads to users based on their browsing behaviour and other data. Fake news sites can attract a large amount of traffic through sensational or misleading headlines and then use programmatic advertising to monetize that traffic. In some cases, the creators of fake news sites may intentionally create false stories or manipulate real news stories to generate clicks and advertising revenue. This is known as click-baiting, and it can be a lucrative business model for those who are willing to sacrifice accuracy and ethics in the pursuit of profit.

Impact of Fake News on Mental Health[4]

The rise of digital media has exposed people to a flood of content, making it challenging to differentiate between real and fake news. Social media platforms are filled with misinformation and disinformation, making it akin to finding a needle in a haystack to uncover genuine news.

The COVID-19 crisis highlighted the importance of accurate information for maintaining a healthy life. Simple measures like handwashing, wearing masks and social distancing held us in good stead through the worst of the pandemic. However, social media was flooded with myths surrounding COVID-19. For example, fake claims that the virus was similar to the flu or that wearing masks was not needed. That it affects only older people and that getting vaccinated could lead to medical complications. These false claims caused a great deal of anxiety and stress for many people who were already worried about the pandemic, leading some to disregard the severity of the virus or dismiss the advice of public health officials.

False information during such life-threatening crises can severely impact people's mental health. Fake news can cause *anxiety and stress* by creating fear and panic, especially when related to catastrophic events or a health scare. This can lead to a feeling of helplessness and loss of control, resulting in increased anxiety. In addition, the constant barrage of conflicting information and sensationalized headlines about a pandemic in the media can also contribute to anxiety and stress. Many people may feel overwhelmed by the sheer volume of news, struggling to discern accuracy. Also, fake news can be *confusing and frustrating*, as it can blur the lines between what is real and what is not. This can lead people to have a distorted view of the world, causing fear, panic, anger or even inciting violence.

It can be designed to provoke *anger and resentment* towards a particular group of people or individuals. This can create a sense of hostility towards others, which can be harmful to mental health. This is because fake news often contains sensationalized, misleading or outright false information that can be used to manipulate people's beliefs and attitudes. When people read or hear fake news that aligns with their pre-existing beliefs, it can further entrench those beliefs and cause them to feel angry or resentful towards those who hold opposing views. This can lead to further division and polarization in society. For instance, a fake news story that blames a certain religious or ethnic group for a terrorist attack can spark widespread outrage and lead to violent attacks against members of that group. In September 2015, a fifty-year-old Muslim man named Mohammad Akhlaq was beaten to death by a mob in the Indian state of Uttar Pradesh over allegations that he had slaughtered and consumed beef in his home. However, it was later revealed that the meat found in his house was actually mutton and not beef. This incident sparked nationwide outrage and raised concerns about communal tensions and the rise of vigilantism in India. Several people were arrested and charged in connection with the murder, including family members of a local politician. The Akhlaq lynching remains a controversial topic in India and has prompted debates around issues of religious intolerance, mob violence and the role of the state in protecting its citizens.

Another case is that of the Tablighi Jamaat, a global Islamic missionary movement that aims to spread the message of Islam and encourage Muslims to practise their faith more effectively. In early 2020, the Tablighi Jamaat found itself at the centre of a controversy in India and other countries due to the COVID-19 pandemic. False information and fake news were spread about the Tablighi Jamaat's role in the spread of COVID-19, particularly in India. Some media outlets and social media users falsely claimed that members of the group deliberately spread the virus or violated lockdown restrictions. These false allegations led to harassment and discrimination against members of the Tablighi Jamaat and fuelled Islamophobia. The Indian government and media outlets later clarified that the Tablighi Jamaat was not responsible for the spread of the virus and that the allegations against the group were baseless. The World Health Organization (WHO) also stated that the Tablighi Jamaat was not responsible for the spread of COVID-19, and that blaming any specific religious or ethnic group for the pandemic was inappropriate and counterproductive.[5]

Similarly, a false story that accuses a particular politician or public figure of corruption or other wrongdoing can lead to angry protests and calls for their resignation or removal from office. In 2016, a false story was circulated online that claimed Hillary Clinton, who was then a presidential candidate, had accepted a bribe from a foreign government. The story suggested that Clinton had sold access to the US State Department in exchange for a donation to her charitable foundation.[6] This story was later found to be fabricated without any factual basis. However, the fake news spread quickly on social media and was picked up by some news outlets, leading to a significant amount of public backlash against Clinton and her campaign. It was later discovered that the false story was created and disseminated by a network of websites and individuals with ties to the Russian government, as part of a broader effort to interfere in the US election and sow discord among the American public.

Fake news can thus have serious real-world consequences, causing harm to individuals and communities and undermining trust in institutions and the media. It is therefore important to be vigilant and to verify information before sharing or acting on it.

Finally, fake news can also contribute to feelings of *depression*, especially if it is about a negative event or situation that is not true. Fake news can contribute to feelings of depression in a number of ways. Firstly, fake news often contains negative and sensationalized information that can be emotionally distressing. For example, fake news stories about natural disasters, terrorism or crime can make people feel anxious, scared and helpless. These feelings can lead to a sense of despair, which can cause depression.

Secondly, fake news can cause people to feel overwhelmed and helpless in the face of a constant barrage of negativity. If people are constantly exposed to fake news stories that highlight problems without offering solutions, they may begin to feel that the world is a hopeless and depressing place. This can lead to a sense of despair and hopelessness, which are also symptoms of depression.

Thirdly, fake news can erode people's trust in the media and in institutions more generally. If people feel that they cannot trust the information they are receiving, they may become more cynical and less engaged with the world around them. This can lead to a sense of disconnection and isolation, which are also risk factors for depression. Overall, fake news can contribute to feelings of depression by creating a sense of overwhelming negativity, eroding people's trust in institutions, and fostering a sense of helplessness and despair. It is important for individuals to be aware of the sources of their news and to seek out reliable information in order to avoid these negative effects.

Media Literacy and Fake News

Media literacy is the ability to access, analyse, evaluate and create media in various forms, such as print, digital and visual media. Media illiteracy, on the other hand, refers to the lack of knowledge, skills or critical thinking abilities needed to understand and navigate media effectively. Media illiteracy can manifest in various ways, such as believing misinformation or propaganda, being unable to identify bias or propaganda in news sources, or being unable to distinguish between credible and unreliable sources of information. It can also lead to a lack of understanding of how media can influence beliefs, attitudes and behaviours. For example, suppose you come across a headline on social media that reads, 'Breaking News: Alien Spaceships Spotted Over New York City'. Without further investigation or verification, you share the post with your friends, and it goes viral. However, after some time, you realize that the news is fake, and the image of the spaceship is photoshopped. This is an example of media illiteracy because you did not critically evaluate or verify the source of the news before sharing it. Media illiteracy can cause misinformation to spread rapidly, leading to confusion and chaos. It is essential to verify the credibility of the news sources and fact-check the information before sharing it.

One example of media illiteracy in India could be the spread of misinformation and fake news through social media platforms. Many people in India, especially in rural areas, have limited access to credible news sources and may rely on social media for information. However, this has led to the circulation of false and misleading information, which can have serious consequences. For instance, during the COVID-19 pandemic, there were numerous instances of misinformation about the virus and its treatment, being circulated on social media. This included false claims that drinking cow urine would cure COVID-19 and that certain herbal remedies could prevent infection. Such misinformation can not only lead to people taking ineffective treatment but can also undermine public health efforts to control the spread of the virus. Another example of media illiteracy is the uncritical acceptance of biased or partisan news sources. Many news channels in India have a clear political bias, and viewers who are not media literate may not be able to distinguish between news and propaganda. This can lead to a polarized and divisive society, where people are more likely to believe what they want to hear rather than what is true.

There is a significant amount of global data available on media literacy, which is the ability to access, analyse, evaluate and create media in various forms. Below are some key findings and statistics related to media literacy worldwide:

1. According to a 2021 UNESCO report, around two-thirds of the world's population is still not connected to the internet and 37 per cent have never used it, and many of those who are connected lack the necessary skills to use it effectively and safely. This digital divide contributes to a lack of media literacy in many parts of the world.[7]

2. The Media and Information Literacy Assessment Framework for Teachers (MIL), developed by UNESCO, found that many students lack critical thinking skills and the ability to evaluate and use

information effectively. The report also found that teachers often lack the training and resources to teach media and information literacy effectively.[8]

3. According to a 2019 survey by the Reuters Institute for the Study of Journalism, only 38 per cent of people in 38 countries trust news media. The survey also found that social media is becoming an increasingly important source of news for many people, but it is also a source of misinformation and propaganda.[9]

4. The European Commission's Eurobarometer survey on media literacy, conducted in 2018, found that only 35 per cent of Europeans have a good level of media literacy. The survey also found that many people lack the skills to identify fake news and that younger generations are often more vulnerable to misinformation online.[10]

5. The Pew Research Center's 2020 survey on Americans' media habits found that social media is the most commonly used source for news, with 55 per cent of Americans saying they get news from social media. However, the survey also found that people who rely on social media for news are less likely to be well-informed and more likely to believe in conspiracy theories.[11]

To combat media illiteracy, it is essential to promote media literacy education and encourage critical thinking skills in evaluating media messages. This can include teaching people how to identify different types of media, assess the credibility of sources and recognize bias in news and advertising. Additionally, it is important to teach people how to create and share media responsibly and ethically. It is an essential skill in today's world, where we are inundated with media messages from multiple sources. However, media illiteracy is becoming increasingly prevalent, leading to misinformation, polarization and other negative consequences. Here are some strategies to combat media illiteracy:

Recognizing Fake News: A study conducted by the Massachusetts Institute of Technology (MIT) in 2018 found that fake news spread faster than real news.[12] Analysing Twitter data between 2006 and 2017, the study found that a fake news story spreads to 1000–100,000 people, whereas accurate news stories reach only 1000 people. Therefore, it is essential to recognize fake news. People need to be taught (starting from school) to read beyond the headline, check the recency of the news and the author's information or the source of news, analyse the tone and language of the news and check the same information from multiple sources to gauge the accuracy and authenticity of the news.

Filtering information from multiple sources: Verifying information through multiple sources is a crucial step in combating fake news. Start with the information you need to verify: it could be a news story, a social media post or any other type of information. Then, look for reputable sources of information that can help you verify the claim. These could include major news organizations, government agencies, academic institutions or non-profit organizations.

Do not rely on just one source to verify the claim. Check multiple sources to ensure that the information is consistent and accurate. If one source contradicts the others, investigate further to determine which source is most reliable. Try to find primary sources that can provide first-hand information on the news. For example, if a news story quotes a study, try to find the actual study to see if the information is accurate. There are many fact-checking websites that can help you verify information. Some of the most well-known ones include Snopes, FactCheck.org, and PolitiFact.

Gauging tone and language: Fake news often uses exaggerated or sensational language to grab the reader's attention and make the story seem more dramatic than it is. It may also use loaded language that is designed to evoke an emotional response from the reader, such as fear, anger or outrage. It may also use language that suggests that the writer has insider knowledge or access to information that is not available to the public. In terms of tone, fake news may adopt a conspiratorial or alarmist tone, suggesting that there is a hidden agenda or a cover-up behind the story. For example, a fake news article might use language like:

- Shocking new evidence reveals the truth about Prime Minister Narendra Modi's graduation degree!
- You won't believe what Aryan Khan did now!
- Experts warn of impending disaster if forest destruction is not stopped!

Always question numbers and figures: When evaluating the accuracy of numbers and figures in a news article, it is important to consider the source of the information and to verify it with other reliable sources. In the case of fake news, the numbers and figures may be deliberately manipulated or fabricated to support a false narrative or agenda. For example, during the COVID-19 pandemic, there were many instances of fake news stories that inflated the number of deaths attributed to the virus. Some fake news stories claimed that the death toll was much higher than official reports. In another case, during the run-up to the 2020 US presidential election, there were instances of election statistics being misrepresented. For example, some fake news stories claimed that a significant percentage of mail-in ballots were fraudulent, while others falsely claimed that the votes of dead people were fraudulently cast.

When it comes to companies, financial data is often manipulated to mislead readers. For example, some fake news stories might inflate the profits or revenue of a company to make it appear more successful than it actually is. A case in point is the infamous Satyam Computers episode, one of the biggest scams in the history of corporate India, in which the account books figures were cooked up and profits were vastly inflated by the promoter. Recently, the Hindenburg report, published by a US-based investment firm on 24 January 2023, made several allegations against the Adani Group, a large Indian conglomerate that operates in various sectors including energy, infrastructure and mining. According to the report, the Adani Group has engaged in several fraudulent practices, including inflating the value of its ports and other infrastructure assets, engaging in circular trading and siphoning money through shell companies. The report also alleged that the group has links to a series of opaque offshore companies that have been used to funnel money out of India. The allegations in the Hindenburg Report resulted in a fall of Gautam Adani's wealth by 60 per cent and by February 2023, the Indian billionaire went from being the world's third richest person to 32nd position, as ranked by Bloomberg.[13] Later even *Signpost*, Wikipedia's independent newspaper, claimed that Adani Group had manipulated Wikipedia entries using fake accounts, creating and revising articles related to the company and Gautam Adani. These accounts were blocked by Wikipedia, it informed.

The power of images: Visual images have a powerful impact on people and this is due to the visual cortex, which is a region of the brain responsible for processing visual information. It is located at the back of the brain, in the occipital lobe, and comprises several different areas that work together to analyse and interpret visual stimuli. When light enters the eye, it is first processed by the retina, which contains specialized cells called photoreceptors that convert light into electrical signals. These signals then travel along the optic nerve to the visual cortex, where they are processed further. Different regions of the visual cortex are responsible for different aspects of visual perception, such as colour, motion, depth and object recognition. For example, the primary visual cortex (also known as V1) is responsible for analysing basic visual features such as edges, lines and contrasts, while higher-level areas such as the inferotemporal cortex are involved in object recognition.

There is evidence to suggest that exposure to fake news can affect the visual cortex. A study published in the journal *Nature Communications* in 2018 found that exposure to fake news can lead to changes in the brain's visual processing regions. The study used functional magnetic resonance imaging (fMRI) to measure brain activity in participants as they viewed real and fake news headlines. The results showed that the participants who were exposed to fake news had increased activity in the visual cortex compared to those who were exposed to real news.[14] This suggests that the brain is processing fake news differently from real news, possibly because it is more novel or unexpected. Overall, the visual cortex plays an important role in processing visual information, and exposure to fake news can affect how the brain processes this information. It is important to be aware of the potential impact of fake news on the brain and to approach news consumption with a critical and discerning mindset. One example of using visual images in fake news is through the manipulation of photos or videos. A fake news article may use a doctored photo or video to support their false claims or mislead the audience. For instance, a photo may be edited to add or remove certain elements, such as people or objects, to create a false narrative or to exaggerate a story. Alternatively, a video may be edited to take statements out of context, alter the sequence of events or even create entirely fabricated events. Another example is the use of misleading or out-of-context images. A fake news article may use a photo that is related to a particular story but is not actually a representation of the event in question. For instance, an article about a protest may use a photo from a different protest, or one that is not even related to protests, to give the false impression that the event was larger or more violent than it actually was.

Digital media stores lots of information, encompassing both real and fake content. If one were to attempt to consume all of the information available on the internet 24x7, it would take approximately 57,000 years. Given the abundance of information, it is imperative that we learn how to discern relevant authentic information while ignoring fake ones. To achieve this, collaboration is required between governments, institutions, digital platforms and individuals to develop digital literacy skills. Digital literacy is essential to combat fake news. With the proliferation of digital media, anyone can create and share content online, and distinguishing between factual information and misinformation can become challenging. Therefore, individuals need to have digital literacy skills to evaluate the credibility and accuracy of information they come across online. Digital literacy involves having a range of skills, such as the ability to navigate digital platforms, assess the reliability of sources and critically analyse information. By developing these skills, individuals can identify fake news and prevent its spread. They can also help others identify fake news by sharing credible sources and fact-checking information, before sharing it.

In conclusion, digital literacy is crucial in combating fake news in today's digital age. By equipping individuals with digital literacy skills, we can create a more informed and educated society that is adept at navigating the complex realm of digital media.

Acknowledgements

Writing a book is a labour of love that requires the support and contribution of numerous individuals. I am deeply grateful to the people who have played a significant role in the creation of this book.

First and foremost, I extend my sincere appreciation to my publisher, Milee Ashwarya, at Penguin Random House India for giving me this opportunity. The insightful feedback and guidance provided by my editor, Manish Kumar Khurana, and copy editor, Aparna Abhijit, have been invaluable in shaping this manuscript. I am also indebted to the entire team at Penguin Random House India for their dedication and hard work in bringing this project to fruition.

I would like to express my heartfelt gratitude to my family for their patience, understanding and support. A source of constant inspiration, they have been the driving force behind my desire to create something meaningful.

It was their encouragement and enthusiasm that kept me going, especially in the moments when self-doubt threatened to derail my progress.

I would also like to express my appreciation to the researchers and experts in the field whose work and insights have informed and enriched the content of this book. To my friends and colleagues, thank you for your unwavering support, encouragement and understanding. Lastly, I want to express my gratitude to the readers. Your enthusiasm for literature and storytelling fuels the creativity of writers like me. Without your support, this book would not have come to life.

Thank you all for being a part of this incredible journey! Your belief in me and this project has been the motivation needed for its completion.

Notes

Chapter I: Fake News—A Guerrilla Communication

1   Oxford Learner's Dictionaries, https://www.oxfordlearners
    dictionaries.com/definition/english/fake-news#:~:text=
    %2F%CB%8Cfe%C9%AAk%20%CB%88nu%CB%
    90z%2F,written%20and%20read%20on%20websites, last
    accessed 6 June 2023.

2   Hugh Harrington, 'Propaganda Warfare: Benjamin Franklin
    Fakes A Newspaper', Journal of the American Revolution,
    10 November 2014, https://allthingsliberty.com/2014/11/
    propaganda-warfare-benjamin-franklin-fakes-a-newspaper/.

3   Taylor Synclair Goethe, 'War, Propaganda and Misinformation:
    The Evolution of Fake News', Reporter Magazine, 26 April
    2019, https://reporter.rit.edu:8443/features/war-propaganda-
    and-misinformation-evolution-fake-news.

4   Collins Dictionary, https://www.collinsdictionary.com/dictionary/
    english/yellow-journalism.

5   Taylor Synclair Goethe, 'War, Propaganda and Misinformation:
    The Evolution of Fake News', Reporter Magazine, 26 April

2019, https://reporter.rit.edu:8443/features/war-propaganda-and-misinformation-evolution-fake-news.

6 Wikipedia, 'Yellow Journalism', Wikimedia Foundation, 26 June 2023, https://en.wikipedia.org/wiki/Yellow_journalism.

7 Sun, Wanning and Minran Liu, 'Red Alert: News Media "Sleep-Walking" into US War Propaganda', Pearls and Irritations, 14 March 2023, https://johnmenadue.com/red-alert-the-danger-of-our-news-media-sleep-walking-into-war-propaganda/.

8 Madeline Halpert, 'War Has Caused $108 Billion in Damage to Ukraine's Infrastructure, Study Finds', *Forbes*, 2 August 2022, https://www.forbes.com/sites/madelinehalpert/2022/08/02/war-has-caused-108-billion-in-damage-to-ukraines-infrastructure-study-finds/?sh=6cd3827923e5.

9 Vladimir Putin, 'On the Historical Unity of Russians and Ukrainians', President of Russia, 12 July 2021, http://en.kremlin.ru/events/president/news/66181.

10 'Russia vs Ukraine: The Fog of Propaganda and Disinformation', Al Jazeera, 4 June 2022, https://www.aljazeera.com/program/the-listening-post/2022/6/4/russia-vs-ukraine-the-fog-of-propaganda-and-disinformation.

11 Joscha Weber, 'Propaganda and Fakes Designed to Manipulate Us', 19 April 2022, https://www.dw.com/en/ukraine-war-how-to-spot-the-propaganda-and-fakes-designed-to-manipulate-us/video-61408681.

12 D.L. Altheide and J.N. Grimes (2005), 'War Programming: The Propaganda project and the Iraq War. *The Sociological Quarterly*, 46(4), 617–43.

13 Foreign & Commonwealth Office, 'Role of Media in Society', GOV.UK, 7 April 2011, https://www.gov.uk/government/speeches/role-of-media-in-society.

14 'Godi Media', Wikipedia, 9 September 2023, https://en.wikipedia.org/wiki/Godi_media#:~:text=Godi%20

media%20(Hindi%20pronunciation%3A%20%5B,NDA%20 government%20(since%202014).

15   Alex Hern, 'Cambridge Analytica: How Did It Turn Clicks into Votes?', *Guardian*, 7 May 2018, https://www.theguardian. com/news/2018/may/06/cambridge-analytica-how-turn-clicks-into-votes-christopher-wylie.

16   Ratan N. Tata, 'This post has neither been said, nor written by me. I urge you to verify media circulated on WhatsApp and social platforms. If I have something to say, I will say it on my official channels. Hope you are safe and do take care', Twitter, 11 April 2020, https://twitter.com/RNTata2000/ status/1248850442030907398?ref_src=twsrc%5Etfw%7Ctw camp%5Etweetembed%7Ctwterm%5E1248850442 030907398%7Ctwgr%5E69b3702ddb6ff6f54117d 36d3530ab2836a55fcc%7Ctwcon%5Es1_&ref_ url=https%3A%2F%2Fwww.hindustantimes. com%2Fit-s-viral%2Fratan-tata-didn-t-write-that-viral-message-attributed-to-him-denies-it-on-twitter%2Fstory-sFOWxXBaBo2EsdtfTTYOYM.html.

17   'Girl seen with Rahul Gandhi in viral pic is not the one who had shouted 'Pakistan Zindabad', Altnews.in, 26 September 2022, https://www.altnews.in/fact-check-rahul-gandhi-bharat-jodo-yatra-amulya-leona-false-claim/.

18   Cecilia Kang and Adam Goldman, 'In Washington Pizzeria Attack, Fake News Brought Real Guns', *New York Times*, 5 December 2016, https://www.nytimes.com/2016/12/05/ business/media/comet-ping-pong-pizza-shooting-fake-news-consequences.html.

Chapter II: Fake News—A Tool for Culture Jamming

1   Dictionary.com, https://www.dictionary.com/browse/culture-jamming, last accessed 8 August 2023.

2   Mark Dery, *Culture Jamming: Hacking, Slashing, and Sniping in the Empire of Signs* (Open Media, 1993).

3   'Billboard Bandits: An Intimate Portrayal of Culture Jamming', Twisted Sifter, 9 May 2012, https://twistedsifter.com/2012/05/billboard-bandits-culture-jammers-photojournal/.

4   'The Polygamy Hoax That Spread from Iraq to Eritrea', BBC News, 30 January 2016, https://www.bbc.com/news/blogs-trending-35430909.

5   Hannah Ritchie, 'Read all about it: The biggest fake news stories of 2016', *CNBC*, 30 December 2016, https://www.cnbc.com/2016/12/30/read-all-about-it-the-biggest-fake-news-stories-of-2016.html.

6   Craig Silverman, 'This Analysis Shows How Viral Fake Election News Stories Outperformed Real News on Facebook', BuzzFeed News, 17 November 2016, https://www.buzzfeednews.com/article/craigsilverman/viral-fake-election-news-outperformed-real-news-on-facebook#.utzB5nez3y.

7   Ibid.

8   Ibid.

9   Teri Finneman and Ryan J. Thomas (2018), 'A family of falsehoods: Deception, media hoaxes and fake news', *Newspaper Research Journal*, 39(3), 350–61.

10 Nicholas Confessore, 'Cambridge Analytica and Facebook: The Scandal and the Fallout So Far', *New York Times*, 4 April 2018, https://www.nytimes.com/2018/04/04/us/politics/cambridge-analytica-scandal-fallout.html.

11 Yusha Rahman, 'Top Six Fake News Stories Shared about Ongoing Farmers' Protests in Delhi', Logical Indian, 7 December 2020, https://thelogicalindian.com/fact-check/farmers-protest-25274.

12 Anmol Alphonso, 'Misinformation Takes Center Stage Around Rahul Gandhi's Bharat Jodo Yatra', BoomLive, 10 September 2022, https://www.boomlive.in/fact-check/politics/fake-news-

round-up-bharat-jodo-yatra-rahul-gandhi-congress-kerala-karnataka-factcheck-19498.

13 Abhimanyu Mathur, 'Did Amber Heard Copy "The Talented Mr Ripley" Lines in Her Testimony? Here's a Fact Check', *Hindustan Times*, 9 May 2012.

14 James Creedon, 'Fake news from the Johnny Depp–Amber Heard defamation trial', France 24, 18 May 2022, https://www.france24.com/en/tv-shows/truth-or-fake/20220518-fake-news-from-the-johnny-depp-amber-heard-defamation-trial.

15 Brijesh Goswami, 'Arjun Kapoor calls report of Malaika Arora's pregnancy "GARBAGE"', Newsroom Post, 30 November 2022, https://newsroompost.com/entertainment/arjun-kapoor-calls-report-of-malaika-aroras-pregnancy-garbage/5212352.html.

16 Brijesh Goswami, 'Arjun Kapoor Calls Report of Malaika Arora's Pregnancy "GARBAGE"', NewsroomPost, 30 November 2022, https://newsroompost.com/entertainment/arjun-kapoor-calls-report-of-malaika-aroras-pregnancy-garbage/5212352.html.

17 'Ranked: Celebrities Most Associated with Fake News', ExpressVPN, 23 May 2023, https://www.expressvpn.com/blog/ranked-celebrities-most-associated-with-fake-news/.

18 'Joe Rogan: Four claims from his Spotify podcast fact-checked', BBC News, 31 January 2022, https://www.bbc.com/news/60199614.

19 'Hrithik Roshan Buys Lavish Apartment to Move in with His Girlfriend Saba Azad before Marriage: Reports', 17 May 2023, https://timesofindia.indiatimes.com/videos/entertainment/hindi/hrithik-roshan-buys-lavish-apartment-to-move-in-with-his-girlfriend-saba-azad-before-marriage-reports/videoshow/100290430.cms; Grace Cyril, 'Kareena Kapoor Debunks Pregnancy Rumours in Hilarious Way, Says "Saif Has Contributed Way Too Much"', *India Today*, 20 July 2022,

https://www.indiatoday.in/movies/celebrities/story/kareena-kapoor-debunks-pregnancy-rumours-in-hilarious-way-says-saif-has-contributed-way-too-much-1977613-2022-07-20.

20 'Ranked: Celebrities Most Associated with Fake News', ExpressVPN, 23 May 2023, https://www.expressvpn.com/blog/ranked-celebrities-most-associated-with-fake-news/.

21 Pierre Berthon, Emily Treen and Leyland Pitt, 'How Truthiness, Fake News and Post-Fact Endanger Brands and What to Do about It', *NIM Marketing Intelligence Review* 10 (1) (20 April 2018): 18–23, https://doi.org/10.2478/gfkmir-2018-0003.

22 Starbucks Coffee (@Starbucks), 'Calling all Starbucks® Rewards members—it's Star Days! We're celebrating you with a week of daily exclusive offers, from 10/18–10/22. Learn more: http://sbux.co/StarDays', Twitter, 18 October 2021, https://twitter.com/starbucks/status/894958528120594433.
Kate Taylor, 'Starbucks shoots down viral rumor that it's giving away free coffee to undocumented immigrants', Business Insider, 7 August 2019, https://www.businessinsider.in/starbucks-shoots-down-viral-rumor-that-its-giving-away-free-coffee-to-undocumented-immigrants/articleshow/59957302.cms.

23 Kate Taylor, 'Starbucks shoots down viral rumor that it's giving away free coffee to undocumented immigrants', Business Insider, 7 August 2017, https://www.businessinsider.in/starbucks-shoots-down-viral-rumor-that-its-giving-away-free-coffee-to-undocumented-immigrants/articleshow/59957302.cms.

24 Starbucks Coffee, 'We're sorry but you've been misinformed. Starbucks is not sponsoring any such event', Twitter, 4 August 2017, https://twitter.com/starbucks/status/894958528120594433.

25 'ITC to file 3rd FIR in Delhi against videos on plastic in 'Aashirvaad Atta', *Economic Times*, 16 March 2018, https://economictimes.indiatimes.com/industry/cons-products/fmcg/

itc-to-file-3rd-fir-in-delhi-against-videos-on-plastic-in-aashirvaad-atta/articleshow/63330038.cms?from=mdr.

26 Hannah Kuchler, 'Companies scramble to combat "fake news"', *Financial Times*, 22 August 2017, https://www.ft.com/content/afe1f902-82b6-11e7-94e2-c5b903247afd.

27 Kim LaCapria, 'Pepsi CEO Tells Trump Supporters to Take Their Business Elsewhere', Snopes, 15 November 2016, https://www.snopes.com/fact-check/pepsi-ceo-tells-trump-supporters-to-take-their-business-elsewhere/.

28 Lamar War Room of Christian for Arizona, 'PepsiCo. CEO to Trump supporters: "We don't want your business" #BoycottPepsi Let's watch stock go down some more', Twitter, 15 November 2016, https://twitter.com/search?q=%23boycottpepsi%20%40lamarwarroom&src=typed_query.

29 'Betteridge's Law of Headlines', Wikipedia, 30 August 2023, https://en.wikipedia.org/wiki/Betteridge%27s_law_of_headlines#:~:text=Betteridge's%20law%20of%20headlines%20is,the%20principle%20is%20much%20older.

30 Hilary Russ, 'Coca-Cola, criticized for plastic pollution, pledges 25% reusable packaging', Reuters, 15 February 2022, https://www.reuters.com/article/coca-cola-vitaminwater-settlement-idUSL1N1211HX20151001.

31 'Airborne Settles Suit over False Claims', NPR, 6 March 2008, https://www.npr.org/templates/story/story.php?storyId=87937907#:~:text=toggle%20caption-,Airborne%2C%20Inc.,companies%20from%20making%20misleading%20claims.

32 'FTC Complaint Charges Deceptive Advertising by POM Wonderful', Federal Trade Commission, 27 September 2010, https://www.ftc.gov/news-events/news/press-releases/2010/09/ftc-complaint-charges-deceptive-advertising-pom-wonderful.

33 Ratna Bhushan, 'Patanjali says didn't claim 'cure' for Covid; Ayush Ministry says Coronil is immunity booster & can't be sold as cure', *Economic Times*, 2 July 2020.

34 'Brands against which ASCI has upheld complaints for misleading advertisement', Retail.com, 5 April 2016, https://retail.economictimes.indiatimes.com/slide-shows/brands-against-which-asci-has-upheld-complaints-for-misleading-advertisement/51700284.

35 Geeta Mohan and Sujeet Jha, 'Lord Ram was Nepali, India set up a 'fake Ayodhya', claims Nepal PM KP Oli', *India Today*, 14 July 2020, https://www.indiatoday.in/india/story/lord-ram-was-nepali-india-set-up-a-fake-ayodhya-claims-nepal-pm-kp-oli-1700220-2020-07-13; 'Rationalist' KS Bhagwan claims Valmiki Ramayana mentions Lord Rama having wine with Sita every afternoon', OpIndia, 21 January 2023, https://www.opindia.com/2023/01/ks-bhagwan-valmiki-ramayana-lord-rama-wine-sita/.

36 Brian Dean, 'WhatsApp 2023 User Statistics: How Many People Use WhatsApp?', Backlinko, 27 March 2023, https://backlinko.com/whatsapp-users.

37 'Can Cow Urine (Gaumutra) Really Cure Cancer?', *Times of India*, 29 April 2019, https://timesofindia.indiatimes.com/lifestyle/food-news/can-cow-urine-gaumutra-really-cure-cancer/photostory/69082518.cms?picid=69082536.

38 'Teach IIT Students About 'Pushpak Viman', Tell Them About Indian Who Invented Plane: MoS HRD Minister Satyapal Singh', *Outlook*, 20 September 2017, https://www.outlookindia.com/website/story/teach-iit-students-about-pushpak-viman-tell-them-about-indian-who-invented-plane/301966.

Chapter III: How Fake News Affects What We Buy and Consume

1 Sumitra Debroy, 'No Excess Lead in Maggi, Maharashtra FDA Says', *Times of India*, 5 June 2015, https://timesofindia.

indiatimes.com/india/no-excess-lead-in-maggi-maharashtra-fda-says/articleshow/47556220.cms.

2   'Ramdev calls Colas Toilet Cleaners', News18, 28 December 2006, https://www.news18.com/news/india/ramdev-calls-colas-toilet-cleaners-254667.html.

3   'Coke sales fall 11% on pesticide controversy', *Business Standard*, 28 October 2003, https://www.business-standard.com/article/companies/coke-sales-fall-11-on-pesticide-controversy-103102901064_1.html.

4   Aroon Deep, 'No more Kurkure jokes! Delhi HC orders posts, tweets to be deleted', Quint, 27 July 2018, https://www.thequint.com/tech-and-auto/tech-news/delhi-hc-pepsico-order-facebook-twitter-blocked.

5   Nick Kindelsperger, 'Scammers Plaguing Chicago restaurants with one-star Google reviews and extortion emails', *Times of Northwest Indiana*, 10 May 2023, https://www.nwitimes.com/news/state-and-regional/crime-and-courts/scammers-plaguing-chicago-restaurants-with-one-star-google-reviews-and-extortion-emails/article_d7b4a57b-1f14-5fdf-beae-e675ba666b28.html.

6   Clara Lindh Bergendorff, 'From The Attention Economy to the Creator Economy: A Paradigm Shift', *Forbes*, 12 March 2021, https://www.forbes.com/sites/claralindhbergendorff/2021/03/12/from-the-attention-economy-to-the-creator-economy-a-paradigm-shift/?sh=1ae70e76faa7.

7   Khusbu Shreshtha, 'Reviews statistics: 50 important online review stats for 2022 [Infographic]', Vendasta, 2 December 2022, https://www.vendasta.com/blog/50-stats-you-need-to-know-about-online-reviews/.

8   'Man jailed in Italy for selling fake TripAdvisor reviews', *Guardian*, 12 September 2018, https://www.theguardian.com/world/2018/sep/12/man-jailed-italy-selling-fake-tripadvisor-reviews-promo-salento.

9   'Twitter campaign takes aim at fake restaurant reviews on Trip Advisor', *Guardian*, 24 October 2015, https://www.theguardian.com/travel/2015/oct/24/twitter-campaign-targets-fake-tripadvisor-restaurant-reviews.

10   Robert Hart, 'Tripadvisor Took Down Nearly 1 Million Fake Reviews Last Year', *Forbes*, 27 October 2021, https://www.forbes.com/sites/roberthart/2021/10/27/tripadvisor-took-down-nearly-1-million-fake-reviews-last-year/.

11   Michael Luca, 'Reviews, Reputation, and Revenue: The Case of Yelp.Com', Harvard Business School, https://www.hbs.edu/faculty/Pages/item.aspx?num=41233.

12   'Amazon sues 1,000 'fake reviewers'', *Guardian*, 18 October 2015, https://www.theguardian.com/technology/2015/oct/18/amazon-sues-1000-fake-reviewers.

13   '18 False Advertising Scandals That Cost Some Brands Millions', Business Insider India, 26 July 2021, https://www.businessinsider.in/advertising/18-false-advertising-scandals-that-cost-some-brands-millions/slidelist/51630710.cms#slideid=51630711.

14   Ratna Bhushan, 'UK Regulator finds Horlicks ad claims too tall', *Economic Times*, 24 October 2008, https://economictimes.indiatimes.com/industry/cons-products/fmcg/uk-regulator-finds-horlicks-ad-claims-too-tall/articleshow/3634861.cms.

Chapter IV: Psychology of Fake News. Why Do People Fall For Fake News?

1   Elyse Samuels, 'How Misinformation on WhatsApp Led to a Mob Killing in India', *Washington Post*, 21 February 2020, https://www.washingtonpost.com/politics/2020/02/21/how-misinformation-whatsapp-led-deathly-mob-lynching-india/.

2   Eryn J. Newman and Lynn Zhang, 'Truthiness: How Non-Probative Photos Shape Belief' in *The Psychology of Fake News* (London, UK: Routledge, 2020), 90–114.

3   Rugile, '30 Fake Viral Photos People Believed Were Real', Boredpanda, 11 July 2023, https://www.boredpanda.com/fake-news-photos-viral-photoshop/.

4   J. Deighton (2008), 'Dove: Evolution of a brand', Harvard Business School Pub, pp. 9–508, https://www.dove.com/us/en/dove-self-esteem-project.html.

5   'What Is Truthiness?', Merriam-Webster, 27 June 2023, https://www.merriam-webster.com/grammar/truthiness-meaning-word-origin#:~:text=Truthiness%20is%20%22What%20I%20say,2006.

6   Brian Duignan, 'Dunning-Kruger Effect | Definition, Examples, & Facts', Encyclopedia Britannica, 18 August 2023, https://www.britannica.com/science/Dunning-Kruger-effect.

7   'Why We Fall for Fake News', Center for Information Technology and Society - UC Santa Barbara, accessed 24 August 2023, https://www.cits.ucsb.edu/fake-news/why-we-fall.

8   Michael Bromberg, 'Illusory Truth Effect: What It Is, Why It Happens, How to Avoid It', Investopedia, 31 May 2023, https://www.investopedia.com/illusory-truth-effect-7488637.

9   'What Is Tejo Mahalaya Controversy?', *Indian Express*, 18 October 2017, https://indianexpress.com/article/what-is/what-is-tejo-mahalaya-controversy-taj-mahal-vinay-katiyar-bjp-4896716/#:~:text=His%20theory%20says%20Taj%20Mahal,renamed%20Taj%20Mahal%2C%20he%20claimed.

10 'Indian WhatsApp Lynchings', Wikipedia, 12 August 2023, https://en.wikipedia.org/wiki/Indian_WhatsApp_lynchings.

11 Parvathi Benu, 'The WhatsApp saga surround JNU attack: Are those viral texts true or false? Here's the truth', Edex Live, 6 January 2020, https://www.edexlive.com/news/2020/jan/06/

the-whatsapp-saga-surround-jnu-attack-are-those-viral-texts-true-or-false-heres-the-truth-9804.html.

12   Munish Chandra Pandey, 'Was Attack on JNU a Pre-Planned Conspiracy? Blame Game Continues', *India Today*, 7 January 2020, https://www.indiatoday.in/india/story/was-attack-on-jnu-a-pre-planned-conspiracy-1634548-2020-01-07.

13   Aditi Chattopadhyay, 'Top Five Fake News Targeting Muslim Community Amid Nationwide Lockdown', The Logical Indian, 10 April 2020, https://thelogicalindian.com/news/islamophobia-covid-19-coronavirus-fake-news-muslim-tablighi-jamaat-20543.

14   B. E. Hilbig (2009), 'Sad, thus true: Negativity bias in judgments of truth', *Journal of Experimental Social Psychology*, 45(4), 983–86. https://doi.org/10.1016/j.jesp.2009.04.012

15   Dan Evon, 'Did Clint Eastwood Refuse the Presidential Medal of Freedom?', Snopes, 23 November 2016, https://www.snopes.com/fact-check/clint-eastwood-and-the-presidential-medal-of-freedom/.

16   Ibid.

17   Mahaprajna Nayak, 'Did Modi Halt Ukraine War for Evacuating Indians? BJP Leaders' Claim Was Refuted by MEA', Alt News, 24 February 2023, https://www.altnews.in/j-p-nadda-falsely-claim-russia-stopped-war-at-pm-modis-phone-call/.

18   Arindam Bagchi, 'All Indian Citizens in Ukraine are advised to not move to any of the border posts without prior coordination with Government of India officials at the border posts (helpline numbers established) and the Emergency numbers of Embassy of India, Kyiv.', Twitter, 26 February 2012, https://twitter.com/MEAIndia/status/1497408184058740738.

19   'Fake news can create tensions, endanger democratic values: CJI Chandrachud', Print, 22 March 2023, https://theprint.in/

india/fake-news-can-create-tensions-endanger-democratic-
values-cji-chandrachud/1464953/.

Chapter V: How Memes Stir Up Fake News

1   Joshua Troy Nieubuurt, 'Internet Memes: Leaflet Propaganda
    of the Digital Age,' *Frontiers in Communication* 5, 15 January
    2021, https://doi.org/10.3389/fcomm.2020.547065.

2   'What Is a Meme?', Grammarly, 20 April 2023, https://www.
    grammarly.com/blog/what-is-a-meme/.

3   'Rahul Gandhi's "Morning Run" Spawns Hilarious Memes
    on the Internet', News18, 31 October 2022, https://www.
    news18.com/news/buzz/rahul-gandhis-morning-run-spawns-
    hilarious-memes-on-the-internet-6277333.html.

4   Kyra Hunting, 'The Role of Popular Media in 2016 US
    Presidential Election Memes,' *Transformative Works and Cultures*
    32, 22 October, 2019, https://doi.org/10.3983/twc.2020.1785.

5   Corey H. Basch et al., 'A Global Pandemic in the Time
    of Viral Memes: COVID-19 Vaccine Misinformation
    and Disinformation on TikTok', *Human Vaccines &
    Immunotherapeutics* 17, no. 8: 2373–77, 25 March 2021, https://
    doi.org/10.1080/21645515.2021.1894896.

6   'Onions Memes & GIFs', Imgflip, https://imgflip.com/tag/
    onions?sort=latest&after=3q2eaf, last accessed 15 September
    2023.

7   Ray's X Owais, 'Rahul Gandhi Hugs Modi Meme | Munna
    Bhai Dubbed', YouTube, 21 July 2018, https://www.youtube.
    com/watch?v=C5o5e_Y8QQY.

8   'चौकीदार ही चोर है।', Facebook, 28 June 2018, https://www.
    facebook.com/Fekunama/photos/2240491405977941.

9   'Election Results 2017: Funny Feku & Pappu WhatsApp
    Messages, Jokes & Images Mock Rahul Gandhi-Akhile',
    India.com, 11 March 2017, https://www.india.com/viral/

election-results-2017-funny-feku-pappu-whatsapp-messages-jokes-images-surface-as-uttar-pradesh-punjab-poll-counting-begins-1914642/.

10 Adrian Willings, 'The Most Famous Internet Memes of All Time', Pocket-Lint, 29 August 2023, https://www.pocket-lint.com/apps/news/140427-best-stupidest-and-most-famous-internet-memes-around/.

11 Don, 'Jet Fuel Can't Melt Steel Beams', Know Your Meme, 11 September 2023, https://knowyourmeme.com/memes/jet-fuel-cant-melt-steel-beams.

12 Alex, 'Wake up Sheeple!', Covid-19 Archive, 26 March 2020, https://covid-19archive.org/s/archive/item/9008.

13 Ana Peraica, 'The Age of Total Images', ResearchGate, 12 December 2019, https://www.researchgate.net/publication/339886861_The_Age_of_Total_Images/figures?lo=1.

14 Nikki McCann Ramirez, 'Trump, Who Wants to Be President, Can't Stop Promoting QAnon Memes', *Rolling Stone*, 23 November 2022, https://www.rollingstone.com/politics/politics-news/trump-qanon-2024-republican-party-1234636195/.

15 'What Is the Great Reset: And How Did It Get Hijacked by Conspiracy Theories?', BBC News, 23 June 2021, https://www.bbc.com/news/blogs-trending-57532368.

16 'Best Funny Liberal Logic Memes', 9GAG, https://9gag.com/tag/liberal-logic/fresh, last accessed 15 September 2023.

17 'Conservative Memes', Pinterest, https://www.pinterest.co.uk/sackesthermcveyagain/conservative-memes/, last accessed 15 September 2023.

18 'Trump Train Memes', Memes Monkey, https://www.memesmonkey.com/topic/trump+train, last accessed 15 September 2023.

19 Mike Ives and Daniel Victor, 'Bernie Sanders Is Once Again the Star of a Meme', *New York Times*, 5 September 2021,

https://www.nytimes.com/2021/01/21/us/politics/bernie-sanders-meme.html.

20 Rob Gallagher and Robert Topinka, 'The Politics of the NPC Meme: Reactionary Subcultural Practice and Vernacular Theory', *Big Data & Society* 10, no. 1: 205395172311724, 1 January 2023, https://doi.org/10.1177/20539517231172422.

21 Aishwarya Upadhye and Archit Mehta, 'General Elections 2019: Memes Flood Social Media after the Results', *The Hindu*, 24 May 2019, https://www.thehindu.com/sci-tech/technology/general-elections-2019-memes-flood-social-media-after-the-results/article27235593.ece.

22 'Main Bhi Chowkidar Memes', Week in Memes, 17 February 2020, https://weekinmemes.com/memes/main-bhi-chowkidar/.

23 Colin Wayne Leach and Aerielle Allen, 'The Social Psychology of the Black Lives Matter Meme and Movement', *Current Directions in Psychological Science*, 26 (6) (15 November 2017): 543–47, https://doi.org/10.1177/0963721417719319.

24 'Fact Check: False Claims about George Soros', Reuters, 29 September 2020, https://www.reuters.com/article/uk-factcheck-false-george-soros-claims-idUSKBN23P2XJ.

25 Maja Brandt Andreasen, 'Not Just a Joke: Rape Culture in Internet Memes about #MeToo', STAX, 2020, https://stax.strath.ac.uk/concern/theses/mg74qm09p.

26 Cassandra Teulon, 'When #MeToo Becomes a Meme', *Observer*, 27 November 2022, https://theobserver-qiaa.org/when-metoo-becomes-a-meme.

27 'Global Daily Social Media Usage 2023', Statista, 29 August 2023, https://www.statista.com/statistics/433871/daily-social-media-usage-worldwide/#:~:text=How%20much%20time%20do%20people,minutes%20in%20the%20previous%20year.

28 Jeff Beer, 'Inside the Secretly Effective–and Underrated–Way Netflix Keeps Its Shows and Movies at the Forefront of

Pop Culture', Fast Company, 1 March 2019, https://www.
fastcompany.com/90309308/by-any-memes-necessary-inside-
netflixs-winning-social-media-strategy.

29 Griffin Kao et al., 'Memes As Marketing', *Turning Silicon
into Gold* (India: Apress, 2020), 99–107, https://doi.
org/10.1007/978-1-4842-5629-9_15.

30 'Meme Marketing 2023: Why Humor And Creativity
Matter', Sprinkles Media, https://www.sprinklesmedia.com/
confectionary/meme-marketing.

31 Angelo Franco, 'The Rise and Fall of the Sassy Brand on Social
Media', Highbrow Magazine, 26 May 2019, https://www.
highbrowmagazine.com/10003-rise-and-fall-sassy-brand-
social-media.

32 Iamdnj, 'Dive into Anything', Reddit, https://www.reddit.
com/r/memes/comments/e1gafd/ever_heard_of_ryan_
reynolds/.

33 'Apple What's a Computer Girl Meme Generator', Imgflip,
https://imgflip.com/memegenerator/122392270/Apple-
Whats-a-Computer-Girl.

34 Tanpreet Kaur, 'Meme Advertising: How E-Commerce
Brands Are Using It (Examples and Practical Tips)', ANS
Commerce, 8 June 2023, https://www.anscommerce.com/
blog/meme-advertising-best-practices-examples/.

35 Ibid.

36 J.C. Anand, 'Amul Girl: An Utterly-Butterly "Meme"-Led
Marketing Legacy Ahead of Its Time,' *Economic Times*, 22
June 2023, https://economictimes.indiatimes.com/industry/
cons-products/fmcg/amul-girl-an-utterly-butterly-meme-led-
marketing-legacy-ahead-of-its-time/articleshow/101192459.
cms?from=mdr.

37 'How Netflix India Uses Digital Marketing Strategy To Win
Customers,' Pepper Content, 13 January 2023, https://www.
peppercontent.io/blog/marketing-strategy-of-netflix/.

38 Nicole Lyn Pesce, 'Burger King Trolls McDonald's with Anti-Happy Meals: "No One Is Happy All the Time"', MarketWatch, 2 May 2019, https://www.marketwatch.com/story/burger-king-trolls-mcdonalds-with-anti-happy-meals-no-one-is-happy-all-the-time-2019-05-02.

39 'Watch Bryan Cranston Spoof "The Shining" in Mtn Dew Super Bowl Ad', Ad Age, 28 January 2020, https://adage.com/article/special-report-super-bowl/watch-bryan-cranston-spoof-shining-mtn-dew-super-bowl-ad/2230906.

40 Al-Muktadir Siam, 'AI and the Future of Modern Memes', Daily Star, 23 January 2020, https://www.thedailystar.net/shout/artificial-intelligence-the-future-of-modern-memes-1857400.

41 IndustryWired, 'Interality Launches "Memeverse" A Virtual World For Memechat', IndustryWired, 12 July 2022, https://industrywired.com/interality-launches-memeverse-a-virtual-world-for-memechat/.

Chapter VI: Role of Media in Spreading Fake News

1 'Tablighi Jamaat Fake News Saga Continues: Arunachal Pradesh Government Calls out Zee News for False Report', Newslaundry, 10 April 2020, https://www.newslaundry.com/2020/04/10/tablighi-jamaat-fake-news-saga-continues-arunachal-pradesh-government-calls-out-zee-news-for-false-report.

2 Anmol Alphonso, 'Aajtak, India.com run fake tweets as Sushant Singh Rajput's last words', Boom, 17 June 2020, https://www.boomlive.in/fake-news/aajtak-indiacom-run-fake-tweets-as-sushant-singh-rajputs-last-words-8511.

3 Jonah E. Bromwich and Ben Smith, 'Smartmatic Files $2.7 Billion Lawsuit against Fox News', New York Times, 4 November 2021, https://www.nytimes.com/2021/02/04/business/media/smartmatic-fox-news-lawsuit.html.

4   Abhishek G. Bhaya, 'Analysis: Was "staged" Gas Attack Footage Used to Bomb Syria?', CGTN, 15 February 2019, https://news.cgtn.com/news/3d3d514d7a457a4e32457a6333566d54/index.html.

5   'SSR Coverage By Republic TV, Times Now 'Contemptuous', Says Bombay High Court', *Outlook*, 19 January 2021 https://www.outlookindia.com/website/story/india-news-media-trial-impacts-probe-bombay-hc-on-sushant-singh-rajput-media-coverage/370982.

6   Siddharth Varadarajan, 'On Kanhaiya: It is Time to Stand Up and be Counted', Wire, 19 February 2016, https://thewire.in/politics/on-kanhaiya-it-is-time-to-stand-up-and-be-counted.

7   Ayush Tiwari, 'How Zee News is trying to prejudice the Delhi riots trials', Newslaundry, 11 September, 2020, https://www.newslaundry.com/2020/09/11/how-zee-news-is-trying-to-prejudice-the-delhi-riots-trials.

8   Arjun Kharpal, 'The Daily Mail has "mastered the art of running stories that aren't true", Wikipedia founder Jimmy Wales says', CNBC, 19 May 2017, https://www.cnbc.com/2017/05/19/daily-mail-jimmy-wales-fake-news-wikipedia-wikitribune.html.

9   Annegret Bieber, 'Fox News: An Analysis of the News Channel's Political Bias' (Examination Thesis, University of Würzburg, 2011).

10   'The Sun admits publishing false story', *Guardian*, 29 December 2010, https://www.theguardian.com/media/greenslade/2010/dec/29/sun-coronation-street.

11   Minimaxir, '30 Linkbait Phrases in BuzzFeed Headlines You Probably Didn't Know Generate The Most Amount of Facebook Shares [OC]', Reddit, 12 January 2015, https://www.reddit.com/r/dataisbeautiful/comments/2s6d1y/30_linkbait_phrases_in_buzzfeed_headlines_you/

12 'Donald Trump Caught Snorting Cocaine in Hotel', Not Allowed To, 20 June 2017, https://notallowedto.com/trump-caught-snorting-cocaine/.

13 Bol Bollywood, 'Salman Khan Caught Drinking In Car Arriving At Party, Hides Glass In Jeans Pocket Seeing Media', YouTube, 3 September 2022, https://www.youtube.com/watch?v=sU0Cp-3FelQ.

14 Smoky Evening, 'Shocking Secrets about Deepika Padukone', YouTube, 6 January 2020, https://www.youtube.com/watch?v=cmLCl67cM7U.

15 Smoky Evening, '10 Bollywood Actress Who Look Shocking Without Makeup | Katrina, Priyanka Chopra, Deepika Padukone', YouTube, 29 January 2020, https://www.youtube.com/watch?v=zihyW8IGzQU.

16 Edward Bernays, 'Propaganda', IG Publishing, 9 January 2004, https://www.igpub.com/propaganda/.

17 'Edward L. Bernays Quotes (Author of Propaganda)', https://www.goodreads.com/author/quotes/275170.Edward_L_Bernays, last accessed 15 September 2023.

18 Richard Gunderman, 'The manipulation of the American mind: Edward Bernays and the birth of public relations', The Conversation, 9 July 2015, https://theconversation.com/the-manipulation-of-the-american-mind-edward-bernays-and-the-birth-of-public-relations-44393.

19 Jessica Lee, 'Did Obama Officials Pressure NBC to Replace Jay Leno?', Snopes, 19 July 2021, https://www.snopes.com/fact-check/obama-jay-leno/.

20 Emily Yahr, 'Jimmy Fallon Tried to Stay out of Politics. But Trump Sucked Him In.', *Washington Post*, 3 December 2021, https://www.washingtonpost.com/news/arts-and-entertainment/wp/2018/06/25/jimmy-fallon-tried-to-stay-out-of-politics-but-trump-sucked-him-in/.

21 Claire Cozens, 'New York Times: We Were Wrong on Iraq', *Guardian*, 15 July 2017, https://www.theguardian.com/media/2004/may/26/pressandpublishing.usnews.

22 Maxim Lott and Charles Couger, 'Draft UN Climate Report Shows 20 Years of Overestimated Global Warming, Skeptics Warn', Fox News, 20 October 2015, https://www.foxnews.com/science/draft-un-climate-report-shows-20-years-of-overestimated-global-warming-skeptics-warn.

23 'News Consumption Trends in India', Statista, 8 September 2022, https://www.statista.com/topics/8332/news-consumption-trends-in-india/#topicOverview.

24 'False News', Transparency Center, 30 September 2021, https://transparency.fb.com/en-gb/policies/community-standards/false-news/.

25 'Synthetic and manipulated media policy', Twitter, April 2023, https://help.twitter.com/en/rules-and-policies/manipulated-media.

Chapter VII: Fake News Amplification

1 Luba Kessler, 'Why Does Fake News Spread Faster than Real News?', *Psychology Today*, 10 April 2018, https://www.psychologytoday.com/us/blog/psychoanalysis-unplugged/201804/why-does-fake-news-spread-faster-real-news.

2 Jim Fournier, 'How algorithms are amplifying misinformation and driving a wedge between people', The Hill, 10 November 2021, https://thehill.com/changing-america/opinion/581002-how-algorithms-are-amplifying-misinformation-and-driving-a-wedge/.

3 Prem Kumar, 'Netflix Movie Recommendation — Using Collaborative Filtering', Medium, 20 March 2020, https://towardsdatascience.com/tensorflow-for-recommendation-

model-part-1-19f6b6dc207d#:~:text=Collaborative%20
filtering%20tackles%20the%20similarities,in%2Dturns%20
does%20the%20recommendations.

4   Larry Hardesty, 'The History of Amazon's Recommendation
    Algorithm', Amazon Science, 1 December 2022, https://www.
    amazon.science/the-history-of-amazons-recommendation-
    algorithm.

5   Soren   Nelson,   'Spotify's   Collaborative   Filtering',
    https://www.math.utah.edu/~gustafso/s2018/2270/
    projects-2018/submittedprojects/sorenNelson/Spotify's%20
    Collaborative%20Filtering.pdf.

6   Dominic Ong, 'Yelp Restaurant Recommendation System—
    Data Science Capstone Project,' Medium, 16 December
    2021, https://towardsdatascience.com/yelp-restaurant-
    recommendation-system-capstone-project-264fe7a7dea1#
    :~:text=Collaborative%20and%20Content%2DBased%20
    Filtering&text=Once%20we%20get%20new%20users,
    return%20the%20highest%20projected%20recommendation.

7   'How YouTube's Recommendation System Works', Particular
    Audience, 24 October 2022, https://particularaudience.com/
    blog/youtube-recommendations/.

8   'Social Media Bots Interview', May 2018, Office of Cyber
    and Infrastructure Analysis, Homeland Security, https://
    niccs.cisa.gov/sites/default/files/documents/pdf/ncsam_
    socialmediabotsoverview_508.pdf?trackDocs=ncsam_
    socialmediabotsoverview_508.pdf

9   'Dark Side of Automation: What You Need to Know about
    Instagram Bots', eZanga, 22 June 2017, https://www.ezanga.
    com/blog/dark-side-of-automation-what-you-need-to-know-
    about-instagram-bots.

10 Lakshmi Varanasi, 'Twitter Bots Appear to Be in Line with the
    Company's Estimate of below 5% - but You Wouldn't Know
    It from How Much They Tweet, Researchers Say', Business

Insider, 9 September 2022, https://www.businessinsider.
in/tech/news/twitter-bots-appear-to-be-be-in-line-with-
the-companys-estimate-of-below-5-but-you-wouldnt-
know-it-from-how-much-they-tweet-researchers-say/
articleshow/94085615.cms.

11 'How Is Fake News Spread? Bots, People like You, Trolls, and
and Microtargeting', Center for Information Technology and
Society, https://www.cits.ucsb.edu/fake-news/spread#spread-
microtargeting, last accessed 15 September 2023.

12 Ibid.

13 'Extremist Content and Russian Disinformation Online:
Working with Tech to Find Solutions', Foreign Policy
Research Institute, 31 October 2017, https://www.fpri.org/
article/2017/10/extremist-content-russian-disinformation-
online-working-tech-find-solutions/.

Chapter VIII: Truth Behind Fake News—Role of Fact-Checkers

1 Saranac Hale Spencer, 'Fake Coronavirus Cures, Part 2: Garlic
Isn't a "Cure"', FactCheck.org, 9 April 2021, https://www.
factcheck.org/2020/02/fake-coronavirus-cures-part-2-garlic-
isnt-a-cure/.

2 'Novel Coronavirus (COVID-19) Deaths by Country
Worldwide 2023', Statista, 29 August 2023, https://www.
statista.com/statistics/1093256/novel-coronavirus-2019ncov-
deaths-worldwide-by-country/.

3 'Transparency,' Snopes.com, https://www.snopes.com/
transparency/, last accessed 15 September 2023.

4 Tanushree Basuroy, 'Exposure to Fake News in India 2019', 26
July 2022, https://www.statista.com/statistics/1027036/india-
exposure-to-fake-news/.

5   'Methodology for Fact Checking', Alt News, 27 June 2018, https://www.altnews.in/methodology-for-fact-checking/.

6   '"Mahatma Gandhi Did Not Have a Single University Degree": J&K L-G Manoj Sinha,' *Indian Express*, 24 March 2023, https://indianexpress.com/article/india/mahatma-gandhi-university-degree-education-jk-manoj-sinha-8516269/.

7   '43 Modi Claims That Are Not True, over 5 Years', Factchecker, 18 April 2019, https://www.factchecker.in/43-modi-claims-that-are-not-true-over-5-years/.

8   Ibid.

9   Eliana Dockterman, 'Trump Inauguration: Crowd Smaller than Obama's.' *Time*, 20 January 2017, https://time.com/4641381/donald-trump-inauguration-crowd/.

10   Jignesh Tiwari and Ayush Patel, 'Truth about 'Sting' Claiming Shaheen Bagh Women Were Paid Rs 500: Alt News-Newslaundry Joint Investigation', Alt News, 6 February 2020, https://www.altnews.in/truth-about-sting-claiming-shaheen-bagh-women-were-paid-rs-500-alt-news-newslaundry-joint-investigation/.

11   Hannah Rashkin et al., 'Truth of Varying Shades: Analyzing Language in Fake News and Political Fact-Checking', *Association for Computational Linguistics* (2017), https://aclanthology.org/D17-1317.pdf.

12   Ibid.

Chapter IX: How to Protect and Defend Yourself from Fake News

1   Stacy Jo Dixon, 'Social Media: Global Penetration Rate 2023, by Region', Statista, 14 February 2023, https://www.statista.com/statistics/269615/social-network-penetration-by-region/.

2   Ibid.

3   Harry Guinness, 'The Real Reason People Share So Much
    Fake News on Social Media', Popular Science, 25 January
    2023, https://www.popsci.com/technology/why-people-share-
    misinformation/.

4   Elianna Lev, 'The Dangers of Disinformation and How
    It Impacts Your Mental Health', Talkspace, 11 January
    2021, https://www.talkspace.com/blog/misinformation-
    disinformation-effect-mental-health/.

5   'Refrain from Religious Profiling of COVID-19 Cases: WHO
    in Context of Tabligh', 7 April 2020, https://www.downtoearth.
    org.in/news/health/refrain-from-religious-profiling-of-covid-
    19-cases-who-in-context-of-tabligh-70262.

6   Katherine Donlevy, 'FBI Dropped 4 Probes into Hillary
    Clinton, Family's Non-Profit Ahead of 2016 Election:
    Durham Report', New York Post, 19 May 2023, https://nypost.
    com/2023/05/18/fbi-dropped-probes-into-claims-clinton-
    accepted-foreign-bribes/.

7   'More than a third of world's population have never used
    internet, says UN', Guardian, 30 November 2021, https://
    www.theguardian.com/technology/2021/nov/30/more-than-
    a-third-of-worlds-population-has-never-used-the-internet-
    says-un.

8   Helen Coster, 'More People Are Avoiding the News, and
    Trusting IT Less, Report Says', Reuters, 14 June 2022,
    https://www.reuters.com/business/media-telecom/more-
    people-are-avoiding-news-trusting-it-less-report-says-2022-
    06-14/.

9   Nic Newman, Richard Fletcher, Antonis Kalogeropoulos and
    Rasmus Kleis Nielsen, 'Reuters Institute Digital News Report
    2019', https://reutersinstitute.politics.ox.ac.uk/sites/default/
    files/2019-06/DNR_2019_FINAL_0.pdf.

10 'Flash Eurobarometer 464: Fake News and Disinformation Online', European Commission, https://data.europa.eu/data/datasets/s2183_464_eng?locale=en.

11 'Pew Research Center's Journalism Project', Pew Research Center, 20 September 2022, https://www.pewresearch.org/journalism/fact-sheet/social-media-and-news-fact-sheet/.

12 Peter Dizikes, 'Study: On Twitter, False News Travels Faster than True Stories', Massachusetts Institute of Technology, 8 March 2018, https://news.mit.edu/2018/study-twitter-false-news-travels-faster-true-stories-0308.

13 'Adani Group: How The World's 3rd Richest Man Is Pulling The Largest Con In Corporate History', Hindenburg Research, 24 January 2023, https://hindenburgresearch.com/adani/.

14 Eveline A. Crone and Elly A. Konijn, 'Media Use and Brain Development during Adolescence', *Nature Communications* 9, no. 1, 21 February 2018.

Scan QR code to access the
Penguin Random House India website